THE POLITICAL ECONOMY OF BREXIT

THE POLITICAL ECONOMY OF BREXIT

Edited by
DAVID BAILEY AND LESLIE BUDD

agenda
publishing

First published in 2017 by Agenda Publishing

Agenda Publishing Limited
The Core
Science Central
Bath Lane
Newcastle upon Tyne
NE4 5TF
www.agendapub.com

ISBN 978-1-911116-63-9 (hardcover)
ISBN 978-1-911116-64-6 (paperback)

British Library Cataloguing-in-Publication Data
A catalogue record for this book is available from the British Library

Typeset by JS Typesetting Ltd, Porthcawl, Mid Glamorgan
Printed and bound in the UK by 4edge Ltd, Essex

CONTENTS

ACKNOWLEDGEMENTS

This volume in part derives from discussions at Brexit: European Dimensions, hosted by Open University's Political Economy Research Group and the Urban and Regional Research Seminar Group held in London in June 2016, shortly before the referendum on the UK's membership of the European Union. We are also grateful to the ESRC's UK in a Changing Europe programme, which funded a one-day workshop at Aston University in late 2015 that fed into the analysis by Bailey and De Propris in this volume. We also wish to thank Alison Howson at Agenda Publishing, who has been a great source of encouragement and ideas. Finally, without the patience of Vanessa and Mikey this volume would never have been completed.

David Bailey
Leslie Budd

CONTRIBUTORS

John Bachtler is professor of European policy studies and a director of the European Policies Research Centre at the University of Strathclyde. His research covers regional and industrial development in Europe, economic development policies, the structural and cohesion policies of the European Union, EU integration and enlargement. He has been an expert adviser to a wide range of governments and European and international organizations, and directs the IQ-Net programme on the management and implementation of structural funds across the EU.

David Bailey is professor of industrial strategy at the Aston Business School. He has written extensively on industrial and regional policy, especially in relation to manufacturing and the automotive industry. He was an area coordinator (on industrial policy) for the FP7 project Welfare, Wealth and Work for Europe (WWWforEurope), and is now participating in MAKERS: Smart Manufacturing for EU Growth and Prosperity, a project funded by the EU Horizon 2020 RISE programme. He is a regular media commentator. A previous chair of the Regional Studies Association, he is now deputy chief editor of the journal *Regional Studies*.

Leslie Budd is reader in social enterprise at the Open University Business School. He is an economist who has written extensively on urban and regional economies in relation to financial markets. His current work focuses on linking city leadership to economic citizenship and governance. He was special economic advisor to the Committee for Enterprise Trade and Investment (CETI) at the Northern Ireland Assembly providing briefings, in particular on the impact of Brexit. He is currently chair of the Urban and Regional Economics Seminar Group (URESG).

Lisa De Propris is professor of regional economic development at the Birmingham Business School and director of its Global Value Chain cluster. Her research interests cover small firms and clusters, competitiveness, innovation, regional development, the knowledge economy and creative and cultural industries. Involved in a range of different funded research projects, she leads the EU Horizon 2020 RISE programme's MAKERS project.

Alex de Ruyter is a professor at Birmingham City University and is head of its Centre for Brexit Studies. He has published widely on regional economic development and labour market issues, with a particular interest in labour market precariousness. He has been involved in a range of funded research programmes, for example as an investigator on the ESRC funded study on the MG Rover closure and its effects on subsequent employment experience of workers.

Jim Gallagher is visiting professor of government at Glasgow University and a research fellow at Nuffield College, Oxford. He is heavily involved in examining the Scottish constitutional question, and is a director in the commercial and charitable sectors. He was Whitehall's most senior civil servant concerned with devolution until he retired in June 2010, as director-general for devolution in the Cabinet Office, the No. 10 Policy Unit, and the Ministry of Justice.

John Milios is professor of political economy and the history of economic thought at the National Technical University of Athens. He has published widely in journals and has authored numerous books, and is director of the quarterly journal of economic theory *Thesseis*. He was chief economic adviser to the Greek leftist party Syriza until March 2015.

Edgar L. W. Morgenroth is an associate research professor at the Economic and Social Research Institute and adjunct professor at Trinity College Dublin. His research interests include transport economics, international trade, economic geography and public economics. He has been analysing the potential impacts of Brexit since 2013 and has published a number of articles and reports on the topic.

Margarita Nyfoudi is a senior lecturer in human resource management at Birmingham City Business School. She is an elected council member of the British Academy of Management, a fellow of the Higher Education Academy, and an associate member of the CIPD. She specializes in multilevel studies, while her research interests include managerial development, workplace learning, leadership and the impact of crises on working conditions.

Tim Oliver is Dahrendorf Fellow for Europe–North American Relations at the London School of Economics and a visiting scholar at New York University. His research focuses on UK politics, UK defence and security policy, UK–EU relations, European geopolitics and transatlantic relations. He has worked in the House of Lords, the European Parliament, the German Institute for International and Security Affairs (Berlin), the SAIS Center for Transatlantic Relations, and the RAND Corporation. He is a non-resident fellow at the SAIS Center for Transatlantic Relations.

Sukhwinder Salh is senior lecturer in employment law and human resource management at Birmingham City University Business School. She is also the course director for the Business and Human Resource Management programme, a chartered member of the CIPD and fellow of the Higher Education Academy. Her research interests include employee relations, cultural identity, equality and diversity and an ageing workforce.

Dimitris P. Sotiropoulos is senior lecturer in finance at the Open University Business School. His research spans the theory of value and money, international political economy and the history of economics, with a particular focus on the political economy of derivatives markets, the social aspects of risk management and the history of financial innovation. Research published work has covered the history of economic thought through to the empirical analysis of the recent Euro area crisis.

Jan Toporowski is professor of economics and finance at the School of Oriental and African Studies, University of London. He specializes in monetary and financial economics and the economics of Michał Kalecki. He has been an active participant in a number of EU-funded projects, including the Financial Integration and Social Cohesion research network and the Financialisation, Economy, Society and Sustainable Development project. He has advised governments and international agencies on banking and monetary policy.

CHAPTER 1

THE POLITICAL ECONOMY OF BREXIT: AN INTRODUCTION

David Bailey and Leslie Budd

In his famous essay *The Eighteenth Brumaire of Louis Bonaparte*, published in 1852, Karl Marx noted that history repeats itself, "once as tragedy, and again as farce". He was referring to Napoleon I and his nephew Napoleon III, with respect to the latter seizing power and implementing a dictatorship in France in 1851. For many the tragedy of Brexit in the UK was followed by the farce of the election of Donald Trump as the 45th president of the United States. The same aphorism could be applied to the Italian Referendum, in which the No vote prevailing led to the resignation of the prime minister, Matteo Renzi. How tragedy and farce will play out in the forthcoming elections in other European countries, especially France and Germany in 2017, is, at the time of writing, anybody's guess, although the defeat of a far-right candidate in the Austrian presidential election may be a cause for some optimism. Some commentators have suggested that the rising nationalist populism in the US and Europe is a sign of the end of the liberal order. Yet this liberal order has brought us increasing inequality, austerity and growing poverty for those people and places early in the twenty-first century. They have been left behind within the great unravelling of the global economy since the global financial crisis that began in late 2007.

But these moments and intervals of shock and fracture are nothing new, especially in Europe. In his masterly study *The Shock of the New: Art and the Century of Change* the Australian art historian Robert Hughes wrote:

> In 1913, the French writer Charles Péguy remarked that "the world has changed less since the time of Jesus Christ than it has in the last thirty years." He was speaking of all the conditions of Western capitalist society its idea of itself, its sense of history, its beliefs, pieties, and modes of production – and its art.
>
> ... After 1914, machinery was turned on its inventors and their children. After forty years of continuous peace in Europe,

the worst war in history cancelled faith in good technology, the
benevolent machine. The myth of the Future went into shock.
And European art moved into years of irony, disgust, and protest.

(Hughes 1991: 9, 56)

It is this context that the decision to leave the EU following the Referendum of
June 2016 can be used to exemplify this "shock" to the polity and economy of
the UK. A similar line of argument has been used to examine the reasons for
the election of Donald Trump in the US and the possible election of far-right
leaders and much larger electoral representation for their parties in France,
Germany, Italy and the Netherlands: in 2017 the "new" in Europe is looking
increasingly like some atavistic shock.

Brexit appears to be treated as a mono-causal event in which the process of leaving should be straightforward enough, given political will and
authority. By the same token, the Leave vote result was merely a factor of
xenophobia combining with the dissatisfaction of people and places left
behind by the EU's globalizing modernity. Yet the electoral geography was
more complex as were the occupational, gender and age differences (Dorling
2016). From this analysis, it was apparent that large swathes of the population voted against something that has increased their economic welfare
in the past or their current economic self-interest. So were these citizens
unintelligent or stupid, falling into the insulting Clinton classification of
"the deplorables"? Clearly not, but the EU may have been crystallized as the
emblem of the status quo of out-of-touch political elites who imposed lower
real wages and worse socio-economic welfare through austerity. In this light,
Leave voters were protesting against the decline in the quality of their lives: a
rational and certainly not deplorable response, but possibly hitting the wrong
target.

This volume seeks to take a multi-dimensional and multi-scalar approach
to the political economy of Brexit. Each of the chapters is set within a wider
context to open discussions on a number of the issues in order to attempt
to make sense of the complexity. The collection does not attempt to cover
all the issues, as there are and will be too many of them, replete with layers
of complexity. It is divided into two parts. The first concentrates on some
key economic dimensions, while the second examines the territorial conundrums thrown up by the challenges of managing and stabilizing the processes of Brexit. Readers will note that there is no chapter on the impact
on Wales. This was deliberate on the part of the editors since the impact of
the Referendum for Scottish Independence and the contiguous land border
between Northern Ireland and the Republic of Ireland make Scotland and
Northern Ireland special cases. It is, however, important to recognize the

importance of all the devolved nations as the trajectory of Brexit proceeds, to which Wales is also likely to play an important role.

We now turn to the first part of the volume.

ECONOMIC DIMENSIONS OF BREXIT

It was clear that during the Referendum campaign both sides displayed considerable ignorance about how modern economies and trade work.[1] The "fear versus fact" discourse meant that a measured analysis of the economic benefits and costs for all UK citizens got lost in this simple dialectic. The claims that there would be an immediate economic catastrophe or that the UK would move immediately into the global economic uplands was expressed by no reasonable economist. Fortunately all the contributors to this volume start from the point of measured expertise. Our first contributor, Edgar Morgenroth, applies his forensic analytical skills in analysing the trade implications of Brexit.

Morgenroth starts "Examining Consequences for Trade: Integration and Disintegration Effects" (Chapter 2) with the proposition that although there is a large literature on the integration effects of trade, there is very little on the disintegration effects. In the opening part of his chapter, Morgenroth uses Algeria and Greenland as examples of disintegration effects following the independence of the former in 1962 and the referendum vote to leave the EU by the latter in 1985. The evidence shows that trade intensity lessens following disintegration, and this is reinforced when the break-up of the former Soviet Union and Yugoslavia is observed. Of closer interest here is the observation that trade intensity lessened by a half following the break-up of Czechoslovakia in to the Czech Republic and Slovakia in 1993. Both became member states of the EU in 2004, with unimpeded tariffs since signing their respective Accession Agreements. A similar pattern emerges for Slovenia and the other former constituent territories of the former Yugoslavia.

In reviewing the evidence of the impact of trade intensity within the wider EU, Morgenroth suggests we should expect to find a positive correlation with

---

1. As has been noted by a number of studies, the potential economic impact of Brexit on the UK economy in the medium term could vary significantly, depending on the form of Brexit (Emmerson *et al.* 2016). Joining the European Economic Area (like Norway) is seen by many as a way of minimizing the costs of Brexit. In terms of other options, a Swiss-style model (with sectoral agreements with the EU) or a Canadian-style trade agreement are seen as better than falling back on World Trade Organization rules (with potential tariff and non-tariff barriers). In short, the more difficult it is for UK-based firms to access the Single European Market then the greater the likely economic cost for the UK over the medium term.

greater integration as the Union expands. This is a reasonable assumption but globalization increases trade with non-EU members so there may be a countervailing tendency. As trade became more globalized, the core EU member states reached a peak in terms of the share of intra-EU trade and then experienced a gradual decline.

In providing a detailed analysis of the impacts of trade in regard to integration and disintegration of EU membership, Morgenroth uses a novel methodology in exploring the potential impact of Brexit in assuming that leaving the EU is symmetric to that of becoming a member. Although there is considerable heterogeneity within the different regions of the UK and within the whole of the EU, Morgenroth concludes that the net impact of Brexit on UK exports to the rest of the EU would be larger by a ratio of nearly eight to one compared to the opposite direction. Furthermore, international trade is closely linked to foreign direct investment (FDI) with the UK having the second largest stock of inward FDI from the EU, after the USA. If the estimates on trade are realized then there may be displacement of FDI from the UK to other parts of the EU.

Jan Toporowski explores the role of finance and the City of London in "Brexit and the Discreet Charm of *Haute Finance*" (Chapter 3). The title relates to the film directed by the Spanish surreal film-maker, Luis Buñuel, *The Discreet Charm of the Bourgeoisie*. One could be forgiven for thinking that the role of finance in the British economy in the past 40 years has been a surreal experience. This is especially the case in its heartland, the City of London, becoming a global offshore finance *entrepôt* that often does not touch but has distorted the real economy. Toporowski uses the work of Karl Polanyi, who identified the relationship between finance and politics in his analysis of the Concert of Europe, a loose coalition of European powers from 1815 until 1823. In seeking to stabilize peace, an anonymous factor began to prevail that dominated the last two-thirds of the nineteenth century and first third of the twentieth: *haute finance*. It functioned as the main link between the political and economic organization of the world during this period.

Toporowski uses a quote from Polanyi to summarize the rise of the Concert of Europe and then asks the reader to replace it with the European Union or the United Nations in respect of the role of global financial markets that are no longer mediated by government or inter-lending global financial governmental agencies. He provides evidence on UK industrial production, showing it to be flat since 1997 with a sharp drop since the global financial crisis of 2008. This decline has created a growing dependence on other sectors to provide employment in the UK. This has not, however reduced the demand for manufactured products and equipment by consumers and businesses. Consequently, there is a growing trade deficit in industrial products reflecting the decline in industrial production while finance has flourished. The decline in industrial production that Toporowski provides evidence for shows the failure of the British government to use *haute finance* as a means of economic revival.

In his view *haute finance* displays discreet charm in that it turns over capital without turning over social structures that were a central consequence of the development of industrial capitalism. This leads him to suggest that the main result of the so-called Thatcher revolution was to hand over the City of London to American interests following "Big Bang" in 1986. Toporowski concludes on the paradox of the UK being a protectorate of US financial interests with low regulatory cost that are a result of the UK's membership of the EU. Thus in promising UK citizens a new place in the world but outside the EU, these US interests may move to other locations within the EU. Doing this would compound the British political elites' failed attempts to address economic decline.

The centrality of industrial decline and restructuring is starting to emerge as the key issue in analysing the impact on the UK economy. Much was made by the Leave campaigners that German car makers will still need to sell their vehicles to buyers in the UK. While this truism is accurate, it hides a lack of understanding of how the automotive sector operates in terms of modern trade. In Chapter 4, "What Does Brexit Mean for UK Automotive Industrial Policy?", David Bailey and Lisa De Propris give an expert account that uncovers the complexity beneath this truism.

Bailey and De Propris begin their chapter by reviewing the star performance of the automotive sector within the UK economy in the last decade. They also point out the benefits for the sector from the UK's membership of the EU in the form of the Single European Market (SEM) access, trade deals with the rest of the world, regulatory influence and access to R&D networks and a skilled labour pool. The key question they address is what Brexit will mean for the sector and its impact upon UK industrial policy.

The short term impacts of Brexit have so far centred on the depreciation of sterling against a number of currencies, especially the euro and the US dollar. This may boost exports of automotive assemblers through cheaper overseas prices but only 40 per cent of UK vehicles' components are locally sourced. Since the depreciation of sterling in late June 2016, imported inflation has risen, increasing the price of foreign-sourced parts and energy costs: the latter priced in US dollars. The resultant lower margins vary across UK-based firms depending upon the scale and scope of local sourcing.

Bailey and De Propris then analyse the impact of Brexit on FDI from two perspectives. First, like many other international trading sectors, vehicle production is fragmented within regionally based global production networks.

Co-ordinating the underlying supply chains and conforming to regulations covering the complex of different components will be more costly after Brexit. Second, much of UK inward FDI is a function of access to the SEM benefiting from a larger market and lower trade costs of being part of a customs union. If the terms of trade are redrawn post-Brexit this may have a detrimental effect on FDI inflows, creating further uncertainty for an already vulnerable global economy in which real investment is at an historic low. Uncertainty undermines investment intentions of all firms, especially those at the heart of cross-border trade and FDI.

The key issue in all this as Bailey and De Propris note is that modern trade is based upon the model of global value chains (GVCs). Within this model a large proportion of trade is intra-firm that incorporates inputs from multiple locations across the globe with each stage creating different levels of value added. Consequently, the critical question is what kind of trade relationship will the UK have post-Brexit? They review a number of alternative scenarios all of which are unsatisfactory for the UK automotive sector. In reviewing firm-specific and other impacts, they observe that upping sticks to another EU location would be costly in the short term due to the problems of double running costs, retooling and logistics.

The turning point occurs with the introduction of new models when factors such as relative UK/EU costs and profits, the volume of imported components and what are alternative production locations in the EU can all be considered by assemblers. Given the uncertainty of what the post-Brexit tariff environment will be then there is a potential risk to UK-based production. The much publicized but opaque deal between the UK government and Nissan over the production of two models remaining in the UK adds to this uncertainty as it is unclear whether such conditions will be extended to other producers, and whether the government will (or indeed can, under World Trade Organization rules) underwrite any costs of changing trade conditions. Other impacts equally apply to other UK sectors, including the loss of influence on regulation; a possible smaller pool of skilled labour due to the ending of free movement within the EU; more limited access to research funds for universities and industry; and the possible ending of European Investment Bank funding to promote low carbon technologies.

In their concluding part, Bailey and De Propris cut to the chase with regard to the role of industrial policy. They review the evidence of successive governments as their attempts to create or undermine a coherent industrial strategy have littered the policy environment. The post-Referendum government led by Theresa May has made a welcome change of tone on industrial strategy; something that is likely to be crucial in the transition from EU membership. The degree to which this becomes successful will depend upon creating a sustainable institutional base. As Bailey and De Propris argue, there is a strong case for "UK industrial strategy to be afforded an institutional status similar to both UK monetary and fiscal policies". In doing so a strong signal would be sent to British industry and foreign investors facing the uncertainties of Brexit.

In "Future Regulation of the UK Workforce" (Chapter 5), Sukhwinder Salh, Margarita Nyfoudi and Alex de Ruyter explore an issue central to the negotiations and outcomes of Brexit, in particular the free movement of labour and the working time directive. The first part of the chapter examines the role of the EU in labour market regulation in the context of a more insecure employment environment. In particular the twin aspects of free movement of labour within the SEM and the European Working Time Directive (EWTD) are used to explore the implications of Brexit. These key issues are picked up in the subsequent section. In the first case, there is an opt-out for the 48-hour maximum working week of which two narratives are attached. Workers can sign an agreement with their employers so as to work above the limit to help make ends meet and give employers more flexibility. The second suggests that the opt-out can lead to exploitation, oppression and an insecure working environment. The issue of holiday and sick leave is one area where pressure on the EWTD has been increased. The directive has been more frequently challenged in the European Court of Justice (ECJ), whose rulings have sometimes added to confusion, as the chapter's authors note. The turbulence that has resulted from inconsistent ECJ rulings led to a review of the EWTD by the previous UK government. A consistent application of the directive is welcome but in the current febrile environment of Brexit and the current government's wish to revoke the authority of the ECJ in the UK, the process and potential outcomes are uncertain.

The free movement of labour is the most contentious and difficult issue as the Brexit negotiating strategy of the current UK government emerges. As the authors observe, maintaining access to the SEM will set up a conflict between the UK and the other EU member states, for whom free movement is a redline. They set out three possible scenarios as the UK leaves the EU, all of which invoke conditions within the current and future visa system. They analyse the system and conditions in a clear and precise manner in the context of the sectoral distribution of the proportion of European Economic Area (EEA) employees in each. The thorny issue of the status of existing EU nationals who work in the UK (and UK nationals in other EU states), which is currently being debated, is assessed using a number of scenarios. Some sectors of the economy will clearly receive more government support in the negotiations over Brexit, in order to gain the benefits of a fuller compromise. At the time of writing, however, the outcomes are too uncertain to call. As

Salh *et al.* note, the UK workforce is facing a highly uncertain future in terms of the impact on its socio-economic welfare arising from the indeterminate nature of Brexit. The authors focus on the sectoral effects, but there is also a strong territorial dimension; this is the subject of Part II of the book.

TERRITORIAL DIMENSIONS OF BREXIT

In this part of the book we draw upon an analysis of the cases of Greece, Scotland, Northern Ireland, EU cohesion policy and the EU as a whole. These cases exemplify what we argue are the territorial conundrums of the process and institutional basis of Brexit whose political economy is multi-dimensional and multi-scalar.

We start with Chapter 6, "The *Exit* Connection: Europe's New Polanyian Moment" by Dimitris Sotiropoulos and John Milios, who draw on the influence of the work of Karl Polanyi to construct their critical narrative. As in Chapter 3, Polanyi's intellectual influence is important in analysing the challenges that moments like Brexit produce. Polanyi's personal life led him from the threat of Nazi persecution from his home in Vienna to the UK where in 1944 he published his best-known work *The Great Transformation* (Polyani 1944). Polanyi attacks market liberalism for what he calls its "stark Utopia". Conservatives had long deployed the "utopianism" epithet to discredit movements of the left, but Polanyi was determined to turn the tables by showing that the vision of a global self-regulating market system was the real utopian fantasy. Polanyi's central argument is that a self-regulating economic system is a completely imaginary construction; as such, it is completely impossible to achieve or maintain. Thus, he provides an important starting point for uncovering the socio-economic and political realities beneath the veil of Brexit as currently constructed.

The authors provide an analysis of the comparison of the threat of Grexit arising from the crisis in the Eurozone and Brexit, and examine the difference and partial similarities with Brexit. They bring a keen outsider's eye in their commentary on the consequences of Brexit, in particular the manner in which the logic of both Grexit and Brexit rests upon a pro-capital labour devaluation strategy. Their opening comments spell out in detail the consequences of a shift back to a 1930s-style laissez-faire (but now irreversible) global economic trajectory.

The authors next explore a central paradox between a post-Brexit UK and a globalizing EU. The paradox centres on the issue of immigration and xenophobia. They examine how anti-immigration was central to the Leave campaign but this is just an extension of the imagined Thatcherite Albion of old. Yet they point out that the rise of far-right anti-immigrant sentiment in all of Europe is not a threat to neoliberalism. The current dominant model of capitalist development is one is which, as Terry Eagleton points out, the commodification of culture and its material benefit recognize no difference in origin, race, sexuality and so on (Eagleton 2016). In this instance Sotiropolous and Milios are providing a version of Toporowski's analysis of the revival of *haute finance*. The Polanyian EU moment in which authoritarian governments result from working political unrest as market society fails to function may be upon us. This possibility is the challenge for the Left in the UK as it tries to negotiate the strategic dilemma of where to position itself in regard to Brexit. Sotiropolous and Milios assess this acute challenge particularly for the current Labour Party leadership. Like the Remain and Leave campaigns, this dilemma challenges the strategic direction of this opposition party whose target should be to improve the working lives of ordinary voters. But for the authors the Party appears unclear about how this should be achieved. Clearly the lessons from outside the UK are useful, for example from Greece, but the authors recognize the context and conjuncture of how different histories are played out.

We return to the UK more directly with Jim Gallagher's "A Scottish Perspective: Charting a Path through the Rubble" (Chapter 7). His opening section provocatively (but rightly) states "what the vote means and what it doesn't mean". He argues that there is a striking resemblance between the nationalist vote in the Scottish Referendum and the Leave vote in the UK-wide EU membership referendum, with the former containing a subtler version of the latter's slogan of "take back control". In this section the author reviews the reason for the success of the Leave vote that creates a conundrum for what the UK should do. As Gallagher notes, the UK government is mandated to pursue Brexit but not through the lens of Nigel Farage's *vie en rose* or Michael Gove's post-truth declaiming.

What the UK government should do is the concern of the next section of Gallagher's chapter, in which he establishes two key questions. First, what is the economic effect of possibly not accessing the UK's biggest market? Second, what will be the overlooked impact on the territorial integrity of the UK and the implications of an exit? He then turns to the argument for remaining part of the EEA that given all the Brexit noise is less fanciful than imagined as the reality of difficult negotiations is more widely understood. The possibility of EEA membership may be the ultimate compromise if the integrity of the UK is not to be undermined. This, as Gallagher observes, may be the minimum condition for the special case of Northern Ireland and the common travel area with the Republic of Ireland (ROI) (see also Leslie Budd's Chapter 8 in this volume). The possibility of an independent Scotland within the EEA thus makes Scotland a special case in the Brexit negotiations: "the tail wagging the dog" perhaps but a potential imperative, if Tom Nairn's vision of *The Break-Up of Britain* is not to be realized (Nairn 1977).

The options for Scotland are then explored in the following sections on what the Scottish government should do, Scotland's interest and options. For Gallagher, Scotland has the advantage of being in two unions: the UK and the EU. Many of the challenges facing the Scottish economy were extensively discussed in the Independence Referendum campaign, and Gallagher points to how losing membership of the SEM in particular would worsen conditions for the economy. In respect of the constitutional options facing a post-Brexit Scotland, possibilities are uncomfortably wide given the general uncertainty and its constitutional special case. But if one constructs a balance sheet it is clear that Brexit is more damaging for Scotland, like Northern Ireland. Any future negotiations over an independent Scotland from a post-Brexit UK opens up a much more complex scenario than that imagined during the Independence Referendum. One imaginative solution that Gallagher offers is to allow the devolved nations to negotiate international treaties with the EU in relation to devolved matters.

The heart of the matter for the devolved nations *and* the regions of the UK is the possibility of a confederated UK. Given the genie of English devolution can no longer be put back in the bottle, this may gain in popularity as the devolved territories may become more powerful. A UK of the nations and regions underwritten by the principle of subsidiarity and by a system of fiscal federalism may be a long way off. Yet the territorial fracturing of the UK is a distinct possibility if the Brexit outcomes lead to a lost decade.

Gallagher concludes by drawing one lesson from the shambles. That is, given the great uncertainty over the timing and outcome of Brexit and what an independent Scotland within or without the EU would look like is there not an opportunity of overcoming the false division between nationalism and unionism?

The question of territorial integrity is at the heart of the potential impact of Brexit on Northern Ireland: a key issue that Leslie Budd takes up in "Stalling or Breaking? Northern Ireland's Economy in the Balance" (Chapter 8). Budd argues that although Northern Ireland punches above its weight politically, it tends to punch below its weight economically. The latter is due to a legacy of conflict, enduring poverty, and the ongoing impact of the global financial crisis exacerbated by the imposition of austerity by the UK government. Yet the economy has enormous potential reinforced by its relationship with the Republic of Ireland that has been one of the most dynamic economies in the EU. However, at the time of the vote to leave the EU, the Northern Ireland economy started to stall as the uncertainty over the outcomes of Brexit took hold. Budd begins by reviewing the performance of the economy to date and how the possibilities of devolved corporation tax (CT) from April 2018 has been undermined. That is, the harmonization of the CT rate with the ROI of 12.5 per cent is touted as stimulating FDI in Northern Ireland. Reducing access to the UK's largest market and its member states, especially the ROI, however, undermines this prospect. Budd advances evidence to show that Northern Ireland will be hit hardest by Brexit unless there are significant compensatory fiscal transfers from the UK government. He then examines the different post-Brexit trade options (including a reformed EU) using the theory of clubs. The argument here is that the different forms of Brexit are club goods (the existing EU, EEA, World Trade Organization, Comprehensive Economic and Trade Agreement) in that they bestow benefits for members at lower cost that excludes outsiders. There comes a point at which the number of members reaches congestion point and the costs of membership rise. From this perspective it is likely that the alternative models on offer will reach the congestion point sooner than existing EU membership.

The other key issue is the border question that opens us a debate about how the common travel area between the two parts of Ireland, established in 1933, will operate post-Brexit. The alternatives of how a hard or soft border misses a fundamental point. There exists a high degree of cross-border co-operation and activities, research and development, trade flows, and joint FDI initiatives. Brexit imposes an economic border in what is a de facto all-Ireland single market that benefits from access to the larger SEM. Thus, as Budd argues, Northern Ireland represents a special case, whose negotiation will be long and very difficult. A Brexit that damages Northern Ireland and the ROI, as in Scotland, opens up the distinct possibility of the territorial disintegration of the UK. Given that Northern Ireland voted to stay in the EU, the possibility of a referendum on reunification of Ireland may not seem so preposterous, as the consequences of leaving EU bear down on Northern Ireland.

The collection now expands its territorial purview in John Bachtler's "Brexit and Regional Development in the UK: What Future for Regional Policy after structural funds?" (Chapter 9). He begins with an overview of the spatial distribution of voting in the Referendum in the context of the regions who will lose funding under the EU's cohesion policy. However, as he points out, the benefit of cohesion policy is a not just funding but provides a stable form of multi-level strategic partnership through its multi-annual programmes. The first section of the chapter provides detailed information and analysis of territorial inequality and the regional distribution of votes between Leave and Remain. The key question of "what have structural funds done for us?" is addressed. Although funding has declined following the expansion of the EU, the UK significantly benefited from this funding stream in regard to its poorer regions and localities. The high point was from the late 1990s until the early 2000s, but as the new millennium wore on EU funding became more prescriptive. The evaluation of the impact of structural funds is variable, partly due to the small size compared to the UK economy but also in terms of unravelling the complex territorial interactions of programmes and local polices. Bachtler provides an expert and insightful analysis of all these issues and in doing so provides a public service to the non-specialist reader.

The key question is what happens to regional policy after structural funds? The post-Referendum government has announced its commitment to a new industrial strategy in which place-based initiatives will be central. But, as Bachtler points out, the proposed government's five-year funding for place-based development is around half that granted by the former regional development agencies (RDAs) in the last programme period. Without a new institutional structure, regional policy and industrial strategy is likely to have limited impact, especially in comparison to our other European neighbours. In conclusion, Bachtler states that Brexit is both a threat but also an opportunity in reforming policy and governance so as to rebalance the most unequal developed economy: a task that may go towards "working for everyone in the UK" post-Brexit.

Brexit is not just a UK process (even if the ROI is included in the negotiation over the complex position of Northern Ireland); it also affects the other member states of the EU profoundly, as Tim Oliver analyses in "What Does Brexit Mean for the European Union?" (Chapter 10). He explores five topics encompassing thirteen Brexit negotiations and debates unfolding in the UK, the rest of Europe and elsewhere. At the end of the chapter Oliver asks if Brexit is a crisis for the EU, European integration and the UK. The five narratives of Brexit that Oliver examines highlight the complexity underlying the dialectic at the heart of the Referendum, but may also be seen as a public expression of the English questioning their place in a seemingly inchoate world.

He then moves onto the EU–UK negotiations in which he amusingly but seriously likens the mantra of "Brexit means Brexit" to a parent's call to a recalcitrant child that "bedtime means bedtime". This metaphor may appear appropriate to the EU negotiators faced with an apparent political and economic immaturity in their UK counterparts. As Jim Gallagher and John Bachtler note in this collection, the territorial integrity of the UK is often overlooked. At the same time, as Oliver notes, diplomacy, security and defence in a post-Brexit universe tends to be downplayed; an irony not missed by a number of strategically important states with global reach. The nub of Brexit is clearly the danger it presents to the rest of the EU in how it will evolve in the range of strategic challenges it faces within and without. In concluding, Oliver asks the question that cuts to the chase of the matter: is Brexit a European Crisis? As in the exposition of other chapters in this connection it challenges the assumption of territorial integrity in two large and still globally important unions. At best Brexit challenges both unions to create new optimal solutions to the current challenges they face. It could be argued that the UK union is a more established and therefore robust one. But the EU was forged in the bitter aftermath of a world conflict that may have more resilience compared to an imagined Arcadian Imperium that many Brexiteers promote. But as Oliver states, politics is the daily management of crisis: the problem is that many UK policy-makers do not consider Brexit to be an EU crisis.

This collection does not dwell on why the British people voted as they did. This has been covered extensively elsewhere, most notably the work of Matt Goodwin (2016). Suffice it to say that the debate to define the Brexit narrative has seen the issue of immigration – rightly or wrongly – take pole position. The British government has therefore set itself the task of restricting continued free movement as part of any deal with the EU, a decision that makes a "hard Brexit" – an exit from the EU's single market – more likely (Wolf 2016).

Whether that future is one where the United Kingdom remains united is a matter that was once again brought to the fore by the EU membership referendum. The Referendum showed that the UK is made of five parts: Scotland, Wales, Northern Ireland, England, and London. Scotland, Northern Ireland and London backed Remain while Wales and England backed Leave. Most debate and analysis has focused on the implications for Scotland, in large part because of the 2014 independence Referendum. Scottish nationalists had, in large part, campaigned for the UK and Scotland to remain in the EU. Independence in the EU has been a key plank of the independence campaign since the 1980s. That the Welsh voted for Leave, and that the Scots are not committed Europhiles, serves as a reminder that Euroscepticism is not confined to the English alone, even if Brexit makes Scottish independence more difficult to implement.

The situation in Northern Ireland often falls off the agenda in Great Britain, with continuing fragility of the peace process and government. Overhanging this is the question of UK–Ireland relations. Ireland's membership of the EU allowed it to emerge from behind Britain, which played a part in making it an equal partner to the UK. Brexit for Ireland poses more questions than for any other EU member state. With the Irish government making clear that it will not be caught in the slipstream of British decisions, despite the potentially significant economic costs for it, Brexit has confronted Ireland with the need to assert its independence, as well as reinforce its position in the EU. The ROI is clearly the fulcrum of how the impact of Brexit in the whole of the EU is negotiated and managed. We in the UK should not underestimate how the history of the EU was forged in conflict but also in compromise.

In finishing, we turn to the great German sociologist, Max Weber, and his twin concept of rationality: formal and substantive. Given the constitution of the UK, the binary choice of the Referendum was hardly in the realm of determinate legal, juridical and constitutional rules and regulations that comprise the former. Given the close result and the territorial distribution of votes based upon a manifold of reasons that cross-cut class, age, gender and ethnicity, the latter type of rationality is hard to divine. As citizens look to representative government to mediate the two types of rationality, the current negotiating stance of the UK government appears to reverse the two types of rationality. What in a sense settles the matter is an appeal to Weber's concept of *Verstehen* (understanding). That is, understanding the meaning of action from the actor's point of view. It is putting oneself in the position of another person as a subject rather than some object of study. It also implies that unlike objects in the natural world human actors are not simply the product of the pulls and pushes of external forces. Individuals are seen to create the world by organizing their own understanding of it and giving it meaning, thereby constructing some form of recognizable but negotiable rationality.

We hope that this volume will contributed to a *Verstehen* of the complex and overlapping rationalities of Brexit, that itself is multi-dimensional and multi-scalar.

REFERENCES

Dorling, D. 2016. "Brexit: The Decision of a Divided Country". *British Medical Journal* **354**: i3965.

Eagleton, T. 2016. *Culture*. New Haven, CT: Yale University Press.

Emmerson, C., P. Johnson & I. Mitchell 2016. *The EU Single Market: The Value of Membership versus Access to the UK*. London: Institute for Fiscal Studies.

Goodwin, M. 2016. "The Brexit Vote Explained: Poverty, Low Skills and Lack of Opportunities". Retrieved from www.jrf.org.uk/report/brexit-vote-explained-poverty-low-skills-and-lack-opportunities (accessed 29 December 2016).

Hughes, R. 1991. *The Shock of the New: Art and the Century of Change*. London: Thames & Hudson.

Marx, K. [1852] 1907. *The Eighteenth Brumaire of Louis Bonaparte* (trans. D. de Leon). Chicago, IL: Charles H. Kerr & Company. Retrieved from https://archive.org/details/theeighteenthbru00marxuoft (accessed 29 December 2016).

Nairn, T. 1977. *The Break-Up of Britain: Crisis and Neonationalism*. London: New Left Books.

Polanyi, K. 1944. *The Great Transformation*. New York: Farrar & Rinehart.

Wolf, M. 2016. "Theresa May Limbers Up for a Hard Brexit". *Financial Times* (20 September). Retrieved from www.ft.com/content/3328547a-7e3d-11e6-bc52-0c7211ef3198 (accessed 29 December 2016).

PART I

ECONOMIC DIMENSIONS OF BREXIT

CHAPTER 2

EXAMINING CONSEQUENCES FOR TRADE: INTEGRATION AND DISINTEGRATION EFFECTS

Edgar L. W. Morgenroth

INTRODUCTION

The decision of the UK to leave the EU runs counter to recent trends towards further integration in most parts of the world. Over recent decades a range of customs unions (CUs), free trade agreements (FTAs) and economic unions (EcUs) have been established and have significantly expanded their membership. These include, among others, the Association of Southeast Asian Nations (ASEAN), the Caribbean Single Market and Economy (CSME), the Gulf Cooperation Council (GCC), the Southern Common Market (MERCOSUR), the North American Free Trade Association (NAFTA), the Commonwealth of Independent States Free Trade Area (CISFTA), the Trans-Pacific Trade Partnership (TTP) and the Eurasian Economic Union (EEU), and their members now account for 153 (80%) of the 192 countries that are members of the United Nations. In addition a large number of proposed agreements are also being negotiated, and indeed a number of countries, such as Turkey, Serbia, Montenegro and Albania, are looking to join the EU.

This increased integration has been both a driver and an effect of globalization. Reduced trade barriers through customs and other economic unions as well as adherence to World Trade Organization rules has made a more fragmented production system possible where inputs are sourced internationally (Feenstra 1998).

While the UK's decision to turn its back on the EU runs counter to the trends of recent decades it is not unprecedented. In 1985 Greenland voted to leave the EU and Algeria, which was an integral part of France, seceded from France in 1962, although that was not a decision against the then EEC.

A number of different existing arrangements between the EU and other countries have been suggested as possible models for the relationship between the EU and the UK. One often cited model is the relationship between Norway and the EU. As this model involves full access to the markets of the EU and the UK respectively it would have the least real economic impact. However, the arrangement between the EU and Norway entails free movement of people and labour, participation in the common external border, accepting almost all EU directives and significant financial contributions by Norway to the EU budget, which means that this arrangement amounts to something resembling EU membership but without voting rights. This is unlikely to be acceptable to UK Eurosceptics after a vote to leave the EU. The arrangement between the EU and Switzerland also involves free movement of people.

Any restriction in the free movement of people by the UK on citizens of the EU is likely to result in the EU restricting access to the EU single market for UK goods and services exports. Given the importance placed by those campaigning for a Brexit on restrictions on the free movement of people, it is therefore likely that trade relations will be less free than the current situation of free trade between the UK and the other member states of the EU. This implies that Brexit is likely to change the trade relationship between the UK and the EU and there will also be consequences for foreign direct investment (FDI), both from outside the EU as well as FDI from EU countries in the UK.

While it is difficult to predict ex-ante what the impact of Brexit will be, as this depends on the outcome of the negotiations between the UK and the EU, it is possible to analyse the impact of previous integration and disintegration effects. In this context this chapter first considers the trade effects of some previous disintegrations, then considers the integration, expansion and glo-balization effects for the UK, Germany and Ireland. The chapter then assess the likely aggregate trade impacts for all EU countries as well as some of the possible impacts on FDI.

DISINTEGRATION EFFECTS

While it is easy to find examples of integration, it is much more difficult to find examples of disintegration. Consequently it is not surprising that the literature has focused on identifying the impacts of integration, which theory argues should be positive (see Panagariyaa & Krishna 2002). The empirical literature is now quite extensive and the most recent papers suggest very substantial trade impacts of being a member of a customs union or free trade agreements on trade with other fellow customs union members. For exam-ple, Baier and Bergstrand (2007) found that the amount of trade between two signatories to a free trade agreement is about double ten years after signing the agreement compared with that expected if the two countries were not signatories.

It is however possible to find a few examples of disintegration. Since the founding of the European Economic Community (EEC) back in 1957 it has expanded and evolved into the European Union (EU). However, even the EEC/EU has lost members in the past. Back in 1962 Algeria, which was an integral part of France, gained independence following a bloody civil war, and was thus no longer part of the EEC.[1] Greenland decided to leave the EU in a referendum held in 1985.

Figure 2.1 shows the impact of Algeria's independence from France on the trade intensity measured as the share of total exports from each country to the other. This measure is chosen as it is difficult to get appropriate export deflators for many countries, and the export share also abstracts from the significant growth of trade volumes in absolute terms.

The graph shows that almost all of Algeria's exports were destined for the French market in the late 1950s, but that the export share accounted for by France declined rapidly following independence. Likewise the substantial share of French exports that were destined for Algeria declined to a marginal share. Of course Algerian independence involved a significant armed struggle and also a significant migrant flow to "mainland" France, with many of the French settlers that formed the backbone of the local economy migrating back to France. This makes this example less relevant for the purposes of assessing the possible impacts of Brexit.

The impact of the referendum in Greenland to leave the EU in 1985 on trade with the EU is shown in Figure 2.2. In addition to trade with the EU the graph also shows exports from Greenland to Denmark and to the EU excluding Denmark. This shows that rather than accounting for less of Greenland's exports the share going to the EU actually increased after the referendum. However, this is accounted for by an increased export share to Denmark and a decreased share of exports going to the rest of the EU. Again this example is unlikely to reflect the impact of Brexit, as Greenland retains close ties with the EU and is regarded as an overseas country and territory because of its political union with Denmark and is still substantially integrated into the internal market and applies EU common external tariffs.

Other examples of disintegration include the break-up of the Soviet Union, Yugoslavia and Czechoslovakia. Fidrmuc and Fidrmuc (2003) analysed the trade impacts of these break-ups, and concluded that "disintegration was followed by a sharp deterioration of bilateral trade intensity". Their results have subsequently been re-examined by de Sousa and Lamotte (2007), who found that while disintegration did lead to reduced trade intensity particularly

---

1. Unlike other French colonies, Algeria was incorporated into France in 1848 and remained a part of France until independence in 1962.

19

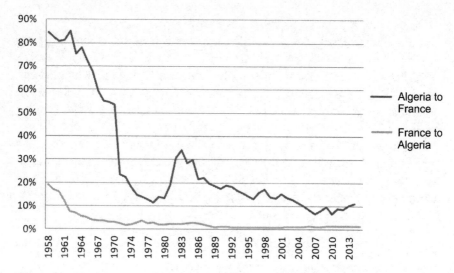

Figure 2.1 Trade intensity between Algeria and France following the breakaway of Algeria (export shares).

Note: The export shares refer to the share of total exports destined to the individual market.

Source: UN Comtrade database.

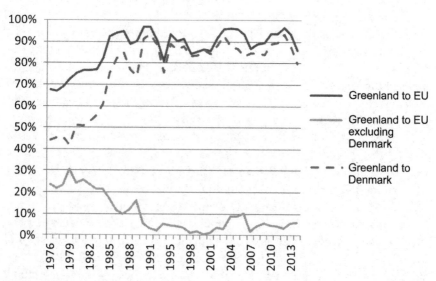

Figure 2.2 Trade intensity between Greenland and the EU (export shares).

Note: The export shares refer to the share of total exports destined to the individual market.

Source: UN Comtrade database.

with respect to Czechoslovakia, this negative trade effect was not universal. However, the period of analysis of both studies is relatively short covering just the years 1993–2001.

A closer examination of the trade intensity over a longer period shows that while not universal, a significant negative impact on trade intensities is observed after disintegration in the case of the former Czechoslovakia, the majority of flows relating to the former Yugoslavia and the Soviet Union. An important dimension to the change in trade patterns among the countries that arose out of the disintegrations is their membership in other or new CUs or FTAs. In particular EU membership seems to have resulted in significant reorientation of trade flows.

Figure 2.3 shows that the trade intensities between the Czech and Slovak Republics declined rapidly following the break-up of Czechoslovakia, despite the fact that trade flows between the two newly formed countries were not impeded by tariff barriers. In just 10 years the trade intensities more than halved. Of course both countries joined the EU in 2004 and were subject to the Accession Agreement signed in 1993.

Yugoslavia broke up successively from 1991 as Croatia and Slovenia declared independence in June of that year, Macedonia declared independence in September, Bosnia-Herzegovina declared independence in March

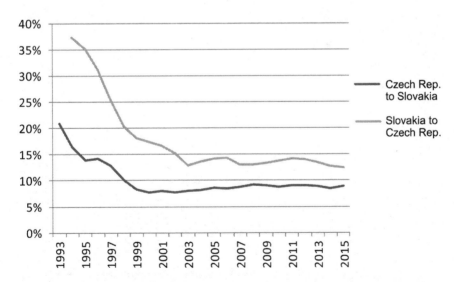

Figure 2.3 Trade intensity between Czech Republic and Slovakia (export shares).

Note: The export shares refer to the share of total exports destined to the individual market.

Source: UN Comtrade database.

1992, Serbia and Montenegro split in May 2006 and finally Kosovo declared independence in February 2008. Given the extended period over which Yugoslavia broke up, data for all trade flows between the countries that made up Yugoslavia is not available over the full period from 1991 onwards, which makes a comprehensive analysis of the trade impacts of this break-up more difficult.

Figure 2.4 shows the impact on export shares from Slovenia. This shows that the export shares declined for exports destined to Macedonia and Montenegro, while the share of Slovenian merchandise exports destined to Bosnia-Herzegovina increased initially but has been on a downward trend since 2002. Slovenian exports to Serbia collapsed shortly after independence and the short armed conflict with what remained of Yugoslavia in 1991, but trade restarted in 1996 albeit at lower levels and the share of Slovenian exports destined to Serbia has been decreasing since 2008 and is now less than half of the original level. The export share to Croatia continuously decreased until 2012 which may well be explained by the fact that Croatia became a member of the EU in 2013. Importantly, Slovenia became an EU member in 2004, which opened up new markets and allowed the country to reorient its trade.

Figure 2.5 shows the export shares for Croatian exports to the countries that formerly made up Yugoslavia. The graph shows that the export share

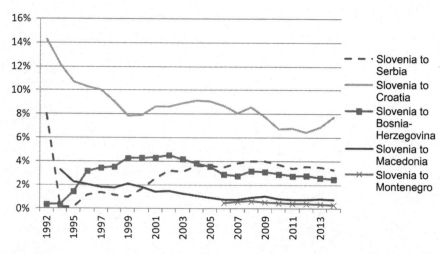

Figure 2.4 Trade intensity between Slovenia and other countries that were formerly part of Yugoslavia.

Note: The export shares refer to the share of total exports destined to the individual market.

Source: UN Comtrade database

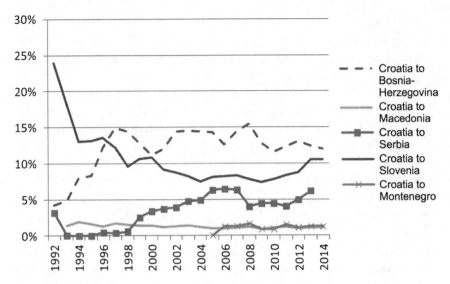

Figure 2.5 Trade intensity between Croatia and other countries that were formerly part of Yugoslavia.

Note: The export shares refer to the share of total exports destined to the individual market.

Source: UN Comtrade database.

to Slovenia declined after independence substantially but has increased more recently as Croatia joined the EU. The share of Croatian exports destined to Macedonia also declined. In contrast, the export shares to Serbia, Montenegro and Bosnia-Herzegovina increased.

EU INTEGRATION AND EXPANSION EFFECTS

As the economies of EU member states integrate with each other one would expect the trade intensity between existing members to increase (i.e. the share of exports accounted for by other EU members should increase). Likewise as the EU expands the share of exports accounted for by EU member countries should also increase. However, globalization which increases trade with non-EU countries should reduce the share of exports among EU member countries. In this section the integration, expansion and globalization effects are analysed for the UK, Germany and Ireland.

Comparing the individual bilateral merchandise export shares when a country joins the EU with that five years after accession shows that this increased in 17 out of 27 countries in the case of the UK, in 20 out of 27 countries for Germany and in 23 out of 27 countries for Ireland. This suggests that there was indeed an integration effect. For the UK, the largest percentage increases in merchandise exports shares five years after joining the EU were recorded for exports to Germany, France and Spain. For Germany the largest percentage increases were recorded for Greece, Spain and Poland and for Ireland the respective destinations were France, Germany and Belgium.

Figures 2.6–2.8 show the merchandise trade intensities with the EU for the three countries as the EU expanded. This shows that there is indeed an expansion effect for both the UK and Germany, but that this has declined with successive expansions. Particularly the last two expansions to include Bulgaria and Romania and Croatia have had very little impact on the share of exports going to the EU, which is not surprising as the three countries have a limited market due to their size and economic development. For Ireland the share of exports accounted for by the EU has been decreasing even though successive expansions have had the effect to provide one-off surges in the share of merchandise exports accounted for by the EU. As is shown in Figure 2.9, where the share of exports accounted for by the EU excluding the UK is shown alongside the share accounted for by the whole EU, this trend is due to a substantial reduction in the share of exports from Ireland to the UK.

The third effect considered here is that of globalization which should reduce the share of exports accounted for by the EU as countries increasingly diversify their export markets. Again, Figures 2.6–2.9 show the trends well. While the share of merchandise exports from the UK accounted for by the EU starts declining in the early 2000s – indicating that from that point other countries are starting to become more important trading partners – for Germany that trend starts considerably earlier and certainly since the mid-1980s. For Ireland, the trend starts in the mid-1990s, which coincides with the significant expansion of mainly US high tech FDI operations in Ireland. This indicates that EU membership has not been an impediment to globalization with 43 per cent of German, 46.8 per cent of Irish and 52.4 per cent of UK merchandise exports destined to non-EU markets.

As the EU expanded and countries globalized more, the share of exports accounted for by the groups of trade partners gradually diminished. For example the share of German exports accounted for by the EU6 countries (Belgium, Germany, France, Italy, Luxembourg and Netherlands) peaked at just over 40 per cent but is now down to just 23.5 per cent, a reduction of 16.6 per cent. The share of German exports accounted for by EU15 countries is also down by 13.2 per cent compared with its peak. For Ireland the shares accounted for by the EU6 and EU15 reduced by 8.2 per cent and 21.5 per cent respectively while for the UK the reductions were 12.8 per cent and 14.4 per cent. This might suggest that expansion and globalization effects for Ireland have impacted less on trade with the EU core countries, than is the case for both the UK and Germany where the impact is more evenly distributed, but this is substantially driven by the reduced export share accounted for by the UK.

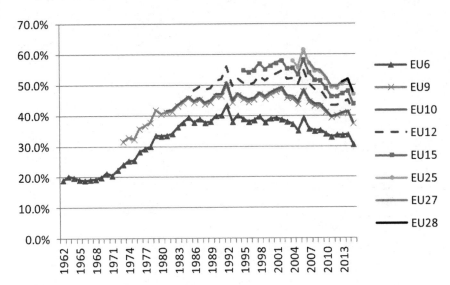

Figure 2.6 UK export shares to the EU.

Source: own calculations using UN Comtrade data.

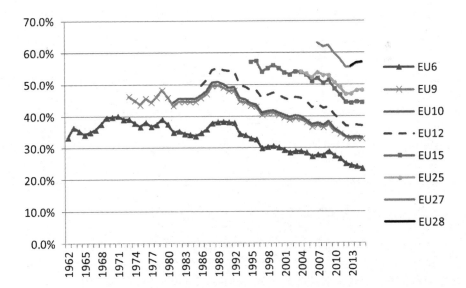

Figure 2.7 German export shares to the EU.

Source: own calculations using UN Comtrade data.

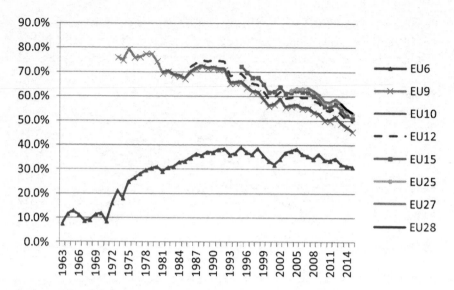

Figure 2.8 Irish export shares to the EU.

Source: own calculations using UN Comtrade data.

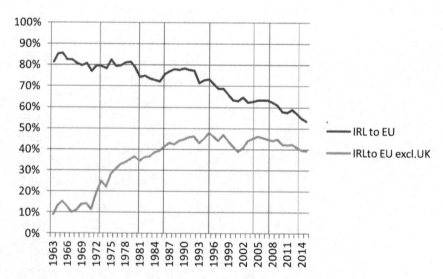

Figure 2.9 Irish export shares to the EU and the EU excluding the UK.

Vertical lines indicate the timing of EU expansions.

Source: own calculations using UN Comtrade data.

POTENTIAL IMPACT OF BREXIT

A simple way to assess the potential impact of Brexit on trade between the UK and the EU is to assume that the impact of leaving the EU is symmetric to that of becoming a member and to take existing estimates of the impact of EU membership on trade flows and assume that these would be reversed. Numerous studies have shown that EU membership increases trade. One comprehensive study which distinguished the impact of different FTAs, CUs and EcUs estimated that EU membership increases trade by about 20 per cent compared to a bilateral trade agreement with the EU (Hufbauer & Schott 2009). This is the approach and set of estimates used previously by Morgenroth (2015), Barrett *et al.* (2015), and Donnellon and Hanrahan (2016).

In 2014, for which the hypothetical effects are calculated, 48.1 per cent of UK merchandise exports and 37 per cent of services exports went to the EU. In contrast just 6.8 per cent of merchandise and 10.4 per cent of services exports from the rest of the EU were destined to the UK. Reducing the trade by the impact identified by Hufbauer and Schott (2009) implies that total UK merchandise and services exports would be reduced by 9.6 per cent and 7.4 per cent respectively, while those from the EU to the UK would be reduced by 1.36 per cent and 2.1 per cent respectively.

Of course the UK trades more with some countries than others and different EU countries trade more with the UK than others, which implies that the impacts on trade flows will not be equal across the individual flows. The impacts by country are shown in Figures 2.10–2.13 and reflect the existing trade shares in 2014. The graphs show that on the merchandise side UK exports to Germany, Netherlands, France, Ireland and Belgium would be most affected while for services Italy replaces Belgium as the fifth most affected flow. For EU countries the most affected for merchandise are Cyprus, Ireland, Netherlands, Belgium and Denmark, and for services they are Ireland, Greece, Luxembourg, Portugal and France.

The results show significant heterogeneity with respect to the impact of Brexit across countries, and it is likely that there is even more heterogeneity across regions. UK regional trade statistics which are produced by HMRC show that 60 per cent of Northern Ireland merchandise exports are destined to the EU market while for the West Midlands that figure is just 40 per cent. Using the same approach as above would indicate that the impact of Brexit on Northern Ireland would be to reduce merchandise exports by about 12 per cent while the merchandise exports of West Midlands would decline by 8 per cent.

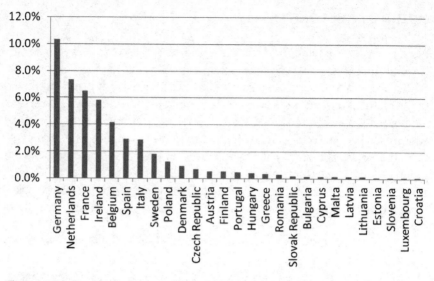

Figure 2.10 Potential impact on UK merchandise to the EU by country of destination.
Source: own calculations using UN Comtrade data

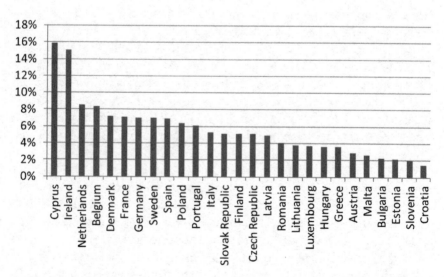

Figure 2.11 Potential impact on EU merchandise to the UK by country of origin.
Source: own calculations using UN Comtrade data

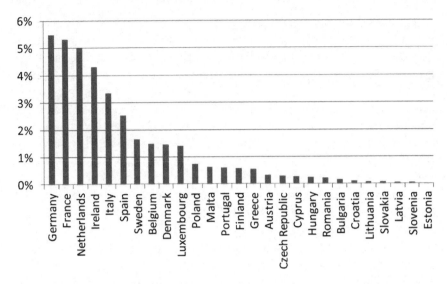

Figure 2.12 Potential impact on UK services to the EU by country of destination.
Source: own calculations using UN Comtrade data

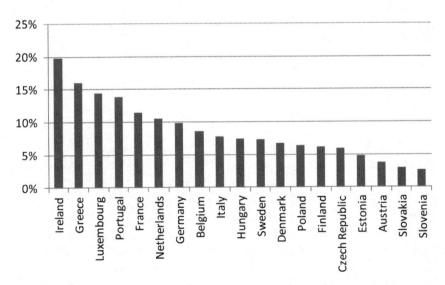

Figure 2.13 Potential impact on EU services to the UK by country of origin.
Source: own calculations using UN Comtrade data

The UK's inward FDI stock is the largest in Europe, and the second largest in the world after the US. Evidence suggests that EU membership has been a key factor in attracting FDI to the UK and Ireland from outside as well as inside the EU (see Hufbauer & Schott 2009). If as discussed above, Brexit leads to trade impediments which imply a loss of market access of UK based firms to the EU, this is likely to reduce FDI in the UK which might divert to other EU members. Of course following Brexit the UK would also be free to take measures that might attract more investment – a reduction of corporation tax rates to 18 per cent has already been announced – other possible measures would be the relaxation of state aid rules or worker protection.

Simulations of the impact of Brexit on the number of new Greenfield FDI projects suggest that a Brexit would more than undo the positive effect of moving to an 18 per cent corporation tax rate in the UK (Barrett *et al.* 2015). For Northern Ireland the results suggest that the effect of a potential reduction of corporation tax to 12.5 per cent would be reversed by a Brexit (*ibid.*). The available analysis suggests that the expected additional attractiveness of Ireland to new FDI projects is likely to be small (*ibid.*). The approach used to assess the trade effects described above can also be applied to FDI stocks using estimates of Hufbauer and Schott (2009). When applied at the aggregate level these estimates suggest that UK FDI would drop by 27 per cent and that of Ireland would increase by about 2 per cent (Morgenroth 2015). Considering the sectoral distribution of FDI in the UK and Ireland the actual effect is likely to be slightly larger, given that a significant share of FDI in the UK is in financial services, which is an industry in which Ireland also has a comparative advantage in.

CONCLUSIONS

This chapter has explored the effects of previous disintegration processes. While none of the examples encompasses the withdrawal of a significant economy from an economic union that is unaccompanied by significant regime changes or armed conflict, they nevertheless provide some useful insights. The analysis shows that disintegration often results in significant changes in trade patterns and reductions in trade with previous partners particularly where alternative partners in CUs, FTAs and EUs exist. In the case of EU members exports are likely to be diverted away from the UK and towards other EU countries if significant trade barriers are introduced post Brexit. For UK exporters the situation would be more difficult as the UK will need to negotiate FTAs which typically takes many years to achieve, and of course FTAs do not necessarily result in totally free trade, as is the case within the EU.[2] This implies that the trade effects will be more negative for the UK than the remaining EU members.

The analysis of previous disintegration effects also suggests that the trade impacts due to disintegration only arise over a longer period of 10 or more years. The distinction between short-term and long-term effects is important. The short-term effects largely relate to uncertainty over the eventual agreement on the future relationship between the EU and the UK, which result in volatility for example in exchange rates and reduced investment. Over the longer term, trade and investment patterns will be affected.

The analysis of the effects of integration, expansion and globalization on the UK, Germany and Ireland showed that the EU expansion increased the share of exports of these countries that was destined to the EU as did EU integration. However, globalization, which reduces the share of exports accounted for by the EU, is starting to dominate the expansion and integration effects. Of course the EU has negotiated a range of trade agreements with 30 other countries, is also provisionally applying six further agreements covering a further 32 countries, and a number of other agreements are waiting to be finalized. This indicates that rather than being a barrier to trading with countries outside the EU, EU membership facilitates such trade.

The analysis of the possible impact of Brexit suggests that the impact on merchandise exports from the UK will be seven times larger than that on merchandise exports from the EU. This reflects the fact that the UK is considerably more dependent on the EU market than the EU (countries) are on the UK market. Of course in the case of the UK, 27 flows would be affected, while for any EU member just one flow would be affected. However, the analysis shows significant heterogeneity of impacts, with some countries hardly being affected while others are more significantly affected.

Loss of market access for UK-based businesses is likely to divert investment, and particularly more mobile foreign direct investment, away from the UK. This would affect both the flow of new FDI into the UK and over the longer term the stock of FDI that is already present in the UK. Importantly, it is likely that any actions by the UK to attract FDI, for example by relaxing state aid rules (see Lawless & Morgenroth 2016a), which would give UK based firms an advantage over EU based firms, are likely to be countered by actions of the EU.

---

2. For example, the negotiations for the Transatlantic Trade and Investment Partnership (TTIP), which have been ongoing since 2013, have not been completed yet. Negotiations on the Comprehensive Economic and Trade Agreement (CETA), which recently concluded, were initiated in 2004.

The focus in this chapter has been on aggregate trade and investment. However, trade is not only unevenly distributed across countries but also across sectors and products. Barrett *et al.* (2015) showed that merchandise trade between the UK and Ireland is highly concentrated in a small number of products. For exports from Ireland to the UK ten products, out of 5,200 in the six-digit Harmonized Standard (HS) product classification, account for over 30 per cent of merchandise exports. Such a concentration of trade in a narrow range of products is also found for other countries. In particular, cars, other vehicles and parts for the car industry constitute a significant share of trade within the EU indicating the fragmentation and integration of production in this sector across the EU. For example 25 per cent of Czech exports to the UK are accounted for by cars and lights for motor vehicles. For the opposite flow five products in the top ten UK exports to the Czech Republic relate to the motor industry and account for 11 per cent of UK exports to the Czech Republic. This concentration of trade implies that if the final agreement between the EU and the UK includes tariff barriers, some sectors are more vulnerable than others (see Chapter 4 of this volume on the automotive industry, for example and Lawless & Morgenroth 2016b for a wider analysis).

REFERENCES

Bair, S. & G. Bergstrand 2007. "Do Free Trade Agreements Actually Increase Members' International Trade?" *Journal of International Economics* **71**(1): 72–95.

Barrett, A., A. Bergin, J. FitzGerald, D. Lambert, D. McCoy, E. Morgenroth, I. Siedschlag & Z. Studnicka 2015. *Scoping the Possible Economic Implications of Brexit on Ireland.* Research Series no. 48. Dublin: Economic and Social Research Institute.

De Sousa, J. & O. Lamotte 2007. "Does Political Disintegration Lead to Trade Disintegration? Evidence from Transition Countries". *Economics of Transition* **15**(4): 825–43.

Donnellan, T. & K. Hanrahan 2016. *Brexit: Potential Implications for the Irish Agri-Food Sector.* Athenry: Teagasc.

Feenstra, R. 1998. "Integration of Trade and Disintegration of Production in the Global Economy". *Journal of Economic Perspectives* **12**(4): 31–50.

Fidrmuc, J. & J. Fidrmuc 2003. "Disintegration and Trade". *Review of International Economics* **11**(5): 811–29.

Hufbauer, G. & J. Schott 2009. "Fitting Asia-Pacific Agreements into the WTO System". In *Multilateralizing Regionalism: Challenges for the Global Trading System*, R. Baldwin & P. Low (eds), 554–635. Cambridge: Cambridge University Press.

Lawless, M. & E. Morgenroth 2016a. "Opportunities and Risks for Foreign Direct Investment". In *Ireland's Economic Outlook: Perspectives and Policy Challenges,*

A. Bergin, E. Morgenroth & K. McQuinn (eds). Forecasting Series EO1. Dublin: ESRI.

Lawless, M. & E. Morgenroth 2016b. *The Product and Sector Level Impact of a Hard Brexit across the EU*. Working paper no. 550. Dublin: ESRI.

Morgenroth, E. 2015. "Economic Consequences for Ireland". In *Britain and Europe: The Endgame*, D. O'Ceallaigh & P. Gillespie (eds), 146–56. Dublin: Institute for International and European Affairs.

Panagariyaa, A. & P. Krishna 2002. "On Necessarily Welfare-Enhancing Free Trade Areas". *Journal of International Economics* **57**(2): 353–67.

CHAPTER 3

BREXIT AND THE DISCREET CHARM OF *HAUTE FINANCE*

Jan Toporowski

THE POWER OF *HAUTE FINANCE*

Over seventy years ago, Karl Polanyi identified the relationship between finance and politics in his observation on the Concert of Europe, the loose coalition of European powers that took over from the Holy Alliance of inter-bred kings and aristocrats, supported in southern Europe by a bureaucracy staffed by Roman Catholic clerics. That Holy Alliance of Austria, Prussia, the Russian Empire and the United Kingdom had put down the revolutionary social movements unleashed by the French Revolution and Bonapartism. The Alliance's successor, the Concert of Europe maintained relative peace in Europe during the near-century after the Congress of Vienna in 1815. The concert, he observed, "lacked the feudal as well as clerical tentacles" of Metternich's Holy Alliance (Polanyi 1944: 9). "And yet", he went on,

> what the Holy Alliance, with its complete unity of thought and purpose, could achieve in Europe only with the help of frequent armed interventions was here accomplished on a world scale by the shadowy entity called the Concert of Europe. For an explanation of this amazing feat, we must seek for some undisclosed powerful social instrumentality at work in the new setting, which could play the role of dynasties and episcopacies under the old and make the peace interest effective. This anonymous factor was *haute finance* …
>
> … Some contended that it was merely the tool of governments; others, that the governments were the instruments of its unquenchable thirst for gain; some, that it was the sower of international discord; others, that it was the vehicle of an effete cosmopolitanism sapping the strength of virile nations. None was quite mistaken. *Haute finance*, an institution sui generis, peculiar

to the last third of the nineteenth century and the first third of the twentieth century, functioned as the main link between the political and economic organization of the world in this period ... While the Concert of Europe acted only at intervals, *haute finance* functioned as a permanent agency of the most elastic kind. Independent of single governments, even of the most powerful, it was in touch with them all; independent of the central banks, even of the Bank of England, it was closely connected with them. There was intimate contact between finance and diplomacy; neither would consider any long-range plan, whether peaceful or warlike, without making sure of the other's good will.

(Polanyi 1944: 9–10)

The end of the gold standard took down with it *haute finance*:

Neither the League of Nations nor international *haute finance* outlasted the gold standard; with its disappearance both the organized peace interest of the League and its chief instruments of enforcement – the Rothschilds and the Morgans – vanished from politics. The snapping of the golden thread was the signal for a world revolution. (Polanyi 1944: 27)

Now if the term "Concert of Europe" in Polanyi's text quoted above is replaced by the terms European Union, or the United Nations, then virtually everything that Polanyi wrote about the discreet, but daily, enforcement power of *haute finance* appears true in the late twentieth and the twenty-first centuries. European summits which decide policy meet four times a year. The European Commission operates all year round but leads on regulation, rather than day-to-day enforcement, while the United Nations operates by consensus with veto powers for the permanent members of its Security Council. But the international financial markets work every day contracting, enforcing and renewing debt and credit structures all over the world. This is not because the world powers have reverted to the gold standard, or anything like it. Rather it seems that, after the interlude of national financial autarchy during the Second World War and under the Bretton Woods system, when international financial transactions were mediated by governments, or inter-government/ multilateral agencies like the International Monetary Fund or the World Bank, banking and financial markets from the 1960s onwards became slowly but cumulatively internationally integrated. This put paid to fixed exchange rates and eventually controls on cross-border movements of capital, which were finally eliminated in Europe at the start of the 1990s.

In truth, Polanyi's ideas of how international finance worked were sugges-
tive but sketchy and incomplete. The very "busy-ness" of such finance, with
daily transactions dwarfing the exchanges necessary for international trade,
or even actual foreign direct investment (see below), had been a notable fea-
ture of international banking before the First World War and remains a challenge even to many financial economists who think banking and finance are
(or should be) about saving and investment, or government finance. Already
in that earlier era of *haute finance*, authors like Hartley Withers, John A.
Hobson (1913)[1] and even John Maynard Keynes knew that the frenzy of daily
activity in the international markets was what provided *liquidity* to otherwise
illiquid long-term financial commitments.

Polanyi thought that cross-border ownership of real or financial assets
was the "peace interest" of international finance, the inter-imperialism of
which Hobson wrote. However, Polanyi (like Lenin) overlooked Hobson's
restriction of this collaboration, between powers with colonial ambitions,
to the Far East of Asia, where Hobson deemed the costs of imperial rivalry
were too great (Hobson [1902] 1938: 311–15). Even more strikingly, Polanyi
appears to have overlooked the catastrophic failure of this "peace interest" in
the First World War, whose financial consequences eventually brought about
the "snapping of the golden thread" of *haute finance*.

Then there is the link of *haute finance* with empire. When Hobson and
Polanyi were writing, Britain had an empire, and it was the wealth of this
empire, in particular the gold reserves of the richest territory in that empire,
India, that allowed the British Government to determine its role and prerog-
atives in the world. With the loss of that empire, the British Government no
longer had the power to decide its role in the world. The fiasco of Anthony
Eden's Suez adventure sixty years ago showed what happened when, as with
the current Brexit policy, the British Government succumbed to global ambitions without global hegemony.

Or, to put it another way, the fact that London is an international financial
centre does not mean that Britain is a global power. There are many international financial centres around the world whose countries of location are not
global powers: Singapore, Tokyo, Frankfurt, Sydney. To understand the scope
and significance of *haute finance* it is necessary to map out the debt structures

---

1. Hobson outlined the relationship between imperialism and *haute finance* in the nineteenth
century. He argued that imperialism adds negligible additional economic advantages to
Britain. But imperialism benefits particular social classes through redistributional effects:
debt to pay for imperial wars redistributes tax revenue to holders of government debt, and
adventurers like Cecil Rhodes were able to count on British military support in enforcing
their predatory claims on territory and resources.

in particular locations. It is such mapping that shows the fragile, perhaps even futile, character of Britain's break for a new global role outside the European Union. In effect the British electorate, or the British Parliament, or the British Crown, may state a preference for a new global role. But they cannot *assume* that role, and *haute finance* will not invest them with it.

THE COMPETITIVENESS OF THE BRITISH ECONOMY

Perhaps the most telling comment that can be made about recent British economic policy, and that can perhaps best illuminate the economic dilemma of a British government determined to find a new place for Britain in the world, is provided by the government's own figures on industrial production over the last two decades. At the start of that period, British industry had recovered more or less to the level of production that it had had before the Thatcher administration had wreaked its "tough love" treatment, of withdrawal of subsidies and closure of loss-making plants, on British industry to make it "competitive" again. The Labour administration from 1997 had dedicated itself to industrial revival through competitiveness by embracing globalization. This was followed by the coalition administration of David Cameron, whose Chancellor of the Exchequer, George Osborne, passed up no opportunity to appear in a hard hat and a high visibility jacket to show his dedication to the industrial revival of the UK. The results of this emphasis on industrial revival can be seen in the diagram below.

As Figure 3.1 shows, industrial production has been essentially flat since 1997, with a long decline in mining and quarrying as oil reserves are run down and coal mines are shut. This decline is compensated by the growth of water and waste management, the fruits of the long-term shift towards recycling and the modernization of what was two decades ago still largely a Victorian water supply system. A visible dip appears in the 2008 financial crisis, and it is clear that, eight years after this event, industry still has not recovered. If we add in the growth of labour productivity, then industrial employment is certainly below what it was in 1997.

The line showing manufacturing production deserves particular note, because this, along with mining, accounts for the bulk of British visible exports. By the summer of the EU referendum, manufacturing had still not recovered the losses due to the 2008 crisis.

The result of this industrial stagnation is a growing dependence on the public sector, transport and communication, and services to provide employment in the economy. However, this has not reduced proportionately the demand of British consumers for manufactured goods, or the demand of firms in the

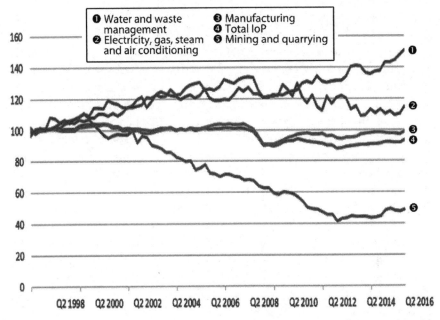

Figure 3.1 Index of production (IoP) and sub-components, Q1 (January–March) 1997 to Q2 (April–June) 2016, UK.

transport and communication and services sectors for industrially-produced equipment with which to conduct their business. Accordingly, Britain continues with a chronic and growing trade deficit in industrial products. The irony is that during these last three or four decades, finance has flourished. What the graph reflects is that finance does not mediate saving with investment, as is commonly thought by economists, politicians and the public, but as Hobson and Keynes discovered, that it makes illiquid financial and real assets, such as real estate and productive machinery, liquid. With every loan against the security of a financial or real asset another layer of credit and debt is added to the economy. In this way money capital may be turned over and earn interest without any actual production taking place.

The graph therefore also reveals the lack of success, of the British government's efforts to use *haute finance* as an instrument of economic revival. The last time that the financial markets were interrogated about their support for British industry was at the end of the 1970s by the Wilson Committee on the functioning of financial institutions (Wilson Committee 1980). The Committee had been set up to head off demands for substantial government control of finance to direct it towards industrial investment. The result was a largely descriptive report concentrating on the benefits that Britain obtains from cross-border trade in financial services, and an emphasis on the pre-Keynesian notion that growing intermediation must make more financial resources (saving) available for investment.

The Conservative government of Margaret Thatcher tried a different tack: the complex cartels that regulated the financial markets were to be swept away in favour of competition. This was done in the 1986 "Big Bang". The outcome was the sale of lowly capitalized British financial firms mostly to US financial conglomerates. This was reinforced under the Labour Administration of Tony Blair which saw an opportunity to make London into the financial centre of the European Union. The outcome was somewhat different. London has indeed become a financial centre of Europe. But it was the American commercial and investment banks, rather than the British government, who made it so. Those banks reserved the long-term capital markets for themselves in America. However, the money markets and the bulk of foreign exchange transactions remained in London. This was not on account of any natural competitive advantage of London, but for the political and geographic reason that Britain is in the European Union, and it is therefore convenient to route dollar–euro transactions (the most common foreign exchange pairing) through London (Lepper *et al.* 2016).

London, as is well-known, is the largest foreign exchange market in the world. That market now turns over something like US$1.2 trillion per day in spot transactions and derivatives. This is almost 200 times the nominal gross domestic product of the UK. However, it is, of course, not production within the UK that these transactions are financing, or even trade between the United States and the European Union as a whole, which these transactions exceed almost 400 times (Bank of England 2016). Rather it is the provision of liquidity against other assets, including financial assets, and derivatives themselves.

Within that total of transactions in London US dollar swaps constitute a distinctive and growing sector. These are short-period swaps of different currencies whose counterparties agree to reverse them, usually at the same exchange rate, at some date in the future. They are distinctive because this is not only a market for foreign exchange. Dollar swaps are also gradually replacing the money markets in Britain and Europe, as, following the crisis of 2008, the sickly remains of those money markets are absorbed into central banks. Over half of the dollar swaps cleared in London's clearing house (LCH Group) are against euros, and only just under a third are in sterling (Stafford 2016).

The obvious precariousness of this situation lies in the possibility that, with Britain's exit from the European Union, this market will migrate to New York or Chicago, where dollar clearing facilities are more readily available, or to a centre located within the European Monetary Union, where euro clearing facilities are more convenient. The majority shareholder in LCH is the London Stock Exchange. Trading dollars in London only makes sense if the dollar swaps market is under the control of US banks able to clear large amounts in US dollars. There is therefore no "independence" of British financial markets outside the European Union. There is only vassalage as an offshore financial centre of the United States expressed in the dependence of the London markets on the monetary cycle in America.

In many respects, the question of the amount of turnover of financial business in London and what that business does for the UK economy is beside the point. As has already been argued, London's financial markets have not done much in the way of financing industrial revival. There is also something deeply Ricardian and unreal about financial reform programmes that suggest that capitalism can be stabilized and made more dynamic by returning the financial system to conditions that existed in the mid-nineteenth century, before the full emergence of *haute finance*. The real problem lies in the relationship of finance to power. This relationship is not only imperilled by the imminent withdrawal of Britain from the European Union. The possibility of that withdrawal is also the consequence of the relationship between finance and politics.

THE DISCREET CHARM OF *HAUTE FINANCE*

Whether in feudal societies with only emergent merchant capitalism, or in our late (or recent) capitalism, finance has two sources of power in relation to sovereigns and governments. The first is the obvious one of being able to supply governments with finance, or liquidity (since my ability to sell a government debt at a good price makes lending to any government worthwhile). The efforts of the European Monetary Union to suppress this capacity to make government debts liquid, because the German government fears residual responsibility for those debts, accounts for the weak development of financial markets in Europe and has contributed to the deflation in Europe. Nevertheless, the possibility, however slim or ephemeral, of that liquidity makes finance powerful throughout the world, especially in those countries that have the institutions that can generate such liquidity, as in Britain, as well as in those countries in Europe most bothered by the absence of such liquidity.

The second source of power for finance is much less visible. Or rather, it is visible not by looking at finance, but at the societies supported by finance. *Haute finance* ingratiates because it turns over capital without overturning social structures. By contrast, industrial capitalism creates a working class that brings with it problems of urbanization and class conflict. Precisely because it

41

is not socially intrusive, *haute finance* is not only compatible with the structures of traditional society. It even gives them a veneer of cosmopolitanism; a halo of modernity around pre-capitalist social structures that one might see in Africa when a farmer uses his mobile phone to check coffee prices in Chicago. This has not to my knowledge been properly investigated by social historians. But it is very apparent in novels such as Anthony Trollope's *The Way We Live Now* or Émile Zola's *L'Argent*, featuring insecure landowners who grasp at finance as a way of repairing family fortunes (Trollope [1875] 1951; Zola [1891] 2009). It perhaps accounts for the "gentlemanly capitalism" that emerged in Britain in the nineteenth century, with roots in landownership, unable after 1914 to break into modern capitalism (Cain & Hopkins 1993), or the industrialization dilemma that afflicts many countries in the Middle East, such as Saudi Arabia, pressed to industrialize in order to provide employment and diversify the economy, but unable to do so without imperilling the traditional norms of social organization.

So it is that in the twenty-first century, members of the Conservative Party from the traditional elite, schooled in the private schools of the English elite and the elite universities of the country, argued among themselves as to who would inherit the political legacy of Margaret Thatcher. She was, of course, the first postwar leader who offered to take Britain back to the nineteenth century and who handed over the City of London to American interests that found traditional society in Britain congenial and established a protectorate over our markets. Those Conservatives resolved their argument by means of a referendum, which wasn't supposed to settle any European issue (and it hasn't) but was to determine who would be the new Thatcher. Thereafter the political difficulties multiplied. In the referendum campaign promises were made to take Britain back to a prelapsarian state in which Britain had few immigrants and our social hierarchies were more secure. Then, unexpectedly, on the 23 June 2016 the electorate voted narrowly to leave the European Union.

The result of the referendum confronts the American protectorate over our financial markets, maintaining in power the elite that has presided over Britain's economic decline, with a dilemma: if Britain takes back from Brussels its powers of regulation over the financial markets, then the British government is, in effect, turning its back on *haute finance*. Any arrangements like those enjoyed by the Swiss, that allow the Swiss financial system to be integrated in the international financial system, leaves powers of regulation in Brussels without much British influence over the scope and content of that regulation. In that case why bother with the British markets when processing financial transactions in New York or Luxemburg may be so much more efficient?

CONCLUSION

Brexit is a political problem for the section of the British political elite who promised during the referendum campaign to give the British people a different place in the world. But people cannot "choose" to have a different place in the world, any more than our African farmer can, by having a mobile, become a capitalist. The concentration of *haute finance* in Britain as an offshore banking centre for the US since 1986 has sustained the British political elite while masking the failure of successive "reforming" British governments since the 1990s to modernize the economy, education and public services. In isolation from the fundamental structural problems of the economy (and society), the narrative around Brexit, justifying or criticizing its economic consequences, misses the most important features of the process of economic decline, which the referendum has accelerated rather than initiated.

In that economic decline, a key part has been played by the location of international financial markets in London, where they have fostered a delusion of British economic and financial "competitiveness". More careful examination of how that financial system has evolved reveals a more complex dependence of Britain's social hierarchy on *haute finance* based in London. That connection to global finance does not change the structural dependence in that system on decisions made in the United States or on the European mainland. A referendum cannot change that, but a traditional ruling elite can throw away its link with modernity.

REFERENCES

Bank of England 2016. "Survey of Foreign Exchange and Over-the-Counter Interest Rate Derivatives Markets". *Bank of England Quarterly Bulletin* 4 (September).

Cain, P. J. & A. G. Hopkins 1993. *British Imperialism: Innovation and Expansion, 1688–1914.* Harlow: Longman.

Hobson, J. A. [1902] 1938. *Imperialism: A Study*, 3rd edn. London: Allen & Unwin.

Hobson, J. A. 1913. *Gold Prices and Wages with an Examination of the Quantity Theory.* London: Methuen.

Lepper, J., M. Shabani, J. Toporowski & J. Tyson 2016. "Monetary Adjustment and Inflation of Financial Claims in the UK after 1980". In *Financialisation and the Financial and Economic Crises: Country Studies*, E. Hein, D. Detzer & N. Dodig (eds), 68–88. Cheltenham: Edward Elgar.

Polanyi, K. 1944. *The Great Transformation.* New York: Farrar & Rinehart.

Stafford, P. 2016. "US Eyes Prize if Swaps Shift from London". *Financial Times* (20 October). Retrieved from www.ft.com/content/8ae3e610-908b-11e6-a72e-b428cb934b78 (accessed 29 December 2016).

Trollope, A. [1875] 1951. *The Way We Live Now.* Oxford: Oxford University Press.

Wilson Committee 1980. *Committee to Review the Functioning of Financial Institutions: Report* ["The Wilson Report"]. Cmnd. 7937. London: HMSO.

Zola, E. [1891] 2009. *L'Argent.* Paris: Flammarion.

CHAPTER 4

WHAT DOES BREXIT MEAN FOR UK AUTOMOTIVE AND INDUSTRIAL POLICY?

David Bailey and Lisa De Propris

The UK's automotive industry has been one of the "star performers" of the UK economy in recent years – unlike many other manufacturing sectors. Output has increased by 60 per cent since 2010 and there has been over £8 billion worth of investment in the industry in the last four years (SMMT 2016a). The industry supports some 800,000 jobs in total in the UK. This upturn has bene-fitted regions, such as the West Midlands which have struggled with deindustrialization, plant closures and the legacy of the global financial crisis (Bailey & Berkeley 2014; Bailey *et al.* 2015; Bailey & de Ruyter 2015). There are many reasons for this recent automotive industry success – the skills base, cooperative working between unions and management, links with universities, a supportive industrial policy and so on. But it should also be noted that a key factor for the success has also been access to the EU single market. Indeed, the industry is seen as having benefitted from EU membership, and not only in accessing the single market, but also through the EU cutting trade deals with the rest of the world, in the UK influencing EU regulations, and in accessing skilled workers and European research funding and networks (KPMG 2014). So what might Britain's departure from the EU mean for the UK automotive sector (hereafter "UK auto"), and in turn for industrial policy in the UK?

This chapter considers short run impacts, before turning to the effect of uncertainty on foreign direct investment (FDI) inflows, firm specific impacts, the nature of a possible trading relationship, and the need for a renewed industrial policy to support UK auto and manufacturing.

SHORT-RUN MARKET AND PRODUCTION IMPACTS

A starting point in understanding the impact of the Brexit vote on the UK auto industry is to consider its impact on the wider UK economy, both in terms of economic growth and the value of sterling. For example, a possible slowdown in economic growth is likely to impact on car sales in the UK, so at best car sales are likely to grow more slowly than otherwise and at worst may fall. For example, PA Consulting forecast a possible fall in UK car sales in the 5–10 per cent range (PA Consulting 2016), while the consultancy firm LMC has revised down its base forecast for the UK's light vehicle market by 15 per cent to 2.55 million units for 2018 (versus 3 million units in 2015) – a reduction in forecast market volume of over 400,000 units for 2018 (LMC 2016a).[1] However, this negative outlook for the auto market may be offset to some extent by the Bank of England's loosening of monetary policy since the referendum (including cuts in interest rates and more quantitative easing), which will help to reduce financing rates on new cars.

With regards to the currency, the value of sterling fell significantly in the aftermath of the Brexit vote (notwithstanding the recovery in its value in late 2016). For UK-based auto assemblers, this depreciation should boost exports. In response to this, firms have a choice between increasing output and increasing prices to raise margins. Nevertheless, this should help boost UK auto output in the short term to over 1.8 million units.[2] So the immediate likely impact on UK auto would seem to be "output up but domestic sales down".

At the same time, however, imported cars and components will become more expensive for the consumer and industry alike. On average, only around 40 per cent of the components that comprise a UK assembled car are sourced locally, as against 60 per cent in Germany (SMMT 2016a), given the nature of fragmented supply chains in UK automotive (Bailey & De Propris 2014). By late 2016 the exchange rate depreciation was already feeding through into inflation, especially in relation to imported components and factory input prices.[3] Such forces will impact on different firms in different ways. Jaguar Land Rover, for example, source a higher proportion of components in the UK and also have higher margins to play with than, say, General Motors through its Vauxhall brand. Both firms have worked hard in recent years to raise their levels of UK sourcing. That could become an imperative if sterling settles down at a lower exchange rate and imported components become too costly.

---

1. In August 2016 GM was the first European producer to announce that it was cutting production in Europe in anticipation of a slowdown of UK car sales. Ford also cut third-quarter European output by over 80,000 units in the wake of the Brexit decision.
2. As noted, a weak UK currency (sterling) might offer an export advantage, if it persists over time, but in low-margin manufacturing such as mass market auto, currency fluctuations may be seen as a negative strategic factor for investors (LMC 2016b).
3. The Office for National Statistics stated in August 2016 that input prices rose 4.3 per cent in July 2016, the first annual increase since September 2013 (*Financial Times* 2016a).

Those auto brands that do not assemble in the UK and only import cars will be negatively affected by the fall in sterling as their cars will become more expensive here (or their margins will be squeezed). So in terms of the auto market in the UK, the "bottom line" is that cars (whether imported or made in the UK) are likely to become more expensive.[4] And a slowdown in economic growth is also still expected for 2018, which will impact on car sales.

UNCERTAINTY AND FOREIGN DIRECT INVESTMENT

There are a number of ways in which Brexit could impact on FDI flows to the UK – whether from the EU or beyond (Dhingra *et al.* 2016; Driffield & Karoglou 2016). First, like other manufacturing industries, car production is fragmented along global value chains of multi-tier suppliers that cross borders and continents. Such value chains are coordinated from strategic locations where the original equipment manufacturers (OEMs) are located and fan out seeking to maximize strategic advantages. Coordinating such supply chains may become more costly with Brexit. Components going into modules that are put together by systems integrators for delivery to final auto assemblers may be subject to different regulations, for example, or be subject to import duties when the UK has left the EU.

Second, FDI flows into the UK have been used as a platform to access the EU single market, with multinationals benefiting from the elimination of tariff and non-tariff barriers. This may change if the terms of trade with the EU are redrawn. Indeed, ongoing uncertainty over the nature of future trading relations between the UK and the EU is likely to affect inward investment in the industry in the UK. Foreign investment has been key to the renewal of the industry, with some £8 billion invested in the sector over the last five years (SMMT 2016a).

As Driffield and Karoglou (2016) note, the biggest single deterrent to foreign investment is uncertainty. The more uncertainty that firms attach to their "net present value calculations", the less likely they are to invest. They note that the single event that caused the greatest decline in inward investment in recent history was Britain leaving the exchange rate mechanism, not because it necessarily implied any particular weakness about the UK economy, but because of the uncertainty that surrounded it. In contrast, they note that the single event that has had the greatest positive impact on inward investment in the UK in recent history was the creation of the single market. This was because it became easier for firms to conduct business within their

---

4. Dhingra *et al.* (2016) suggest that UK car prices could rise by 2.5 per cent after Brexit.

organization across national borders. For example, automotive and engine assemblers like GM, BMW and Ford all import sizeable inflows of components to the UK from their other EU operations and from the broader value chain.

The key point here is that trade is no longer bilateral between countries; rather trade is characterized by fine grained cross-border value chains where the end product incorporates inputs from multiple origins. Indeed, industrial production today occurs through the veins of global production networks (Coe & Yeung 2015) that span borders and are headed by multinationals (some of which are starting to originate from emerging economies such as China; Matthews 2006). The global value chain (GVC) model suggests that not all stages of production contribute with the same value added to the final product (Gereffi *et al.* 2005). As KPMG (2014) illustrate, a typical driveline system produced by GKN, the British-based supplier of automotive driveline technologies and systems, incorporates specialist forged parts from Spain, Italy, France and Germany which are then assembled at GKN Driveline's UK factory and supplied to automotive assemblers in the UK and EU. This is illustrated in Figure 4.1. The components, assembled drivelines and the then final assembled car could cross the English Channel several times.

As noted above, these value chains need to be "frictionless" in terms of non-tariff barriers (think of regulations and standards) as well as tariffs. As KPMG noted before the vote:

> Original equipment manufacturers such as aircraft and automotive manufacturers could perhaps favour the simplicity and flexibility of an EU-supply base rather than dealing with the potential complexities of a company based outside the union. In the long term, more EU-based alternatives would emerge. As buyers churned their suppliers, UK firms might become more marginalized. The integration of supply chains is a double edged sword – our manufacturers are not indispensable.   (KPMG 2016: 13)

Anything which puts these value chain relationships at risk, whether currency risk or higher transactions costs from having to deal with EU and UK regulations separately, reduces the likelihood of further investment. As Driffield and Karoglou (2016) note, if one looks at past events in terms of magnitude, Brexit may have a short-term negative shock on inward investment. They suggest that it would then take about 4 years for the UK to get back to a new lower long-term trend of inward investment.

The trade issue is also critical as over 80 per cent of cars assembled in the UK are exported, and over 50 per cent of these exports go to Europe

done.[5] Yet completely free trade on all goods and services (as now) *but without* paying into the EU budget or agreeing to the free movement of people is probably going to be a non-starter. A deal will have to be done, but the compromise will take some time to sort out, and that uncertainty is itself a major risk in terms of inward foreign investment in the auto industry. So there is uncertainty, and industry is uncertain as to how long it will go on.

As Holmes (2016) notes, there are practical difficulties to be overcome with sectoral deals for industries like auto. A full free trade agreement (FTA) would make exported cars free of tariffs into the EU, but to benefit from this they need to meet the EU's FTA rules of origin. Currently, these require 60 per cent of a car's value added to be "local" to benefit from the FTA (or with parts and components from the EU under a so-called "cumulation" agreement). So to eliminate border bureaucracy there would need to be a customs union arrangement and a mutual recognition agreement for conformity assessment. However, to ensure automatic mutual recognition of the UK's conformity assessment, EEA states have to accept supranational enforcement. This could violate a UK "red line" in Brexit talks. One possibility would be to sign a special FTA in which agreement in which both sides agreed that in industries where the UK keeps the same external tariffs as the EU's common external tariff then rules of origin would not be checked. As Holmes (*ibid.*) notes, such a deal is imaginable in cars because both sides have an interest in maintaining value chains in the sector.

FIRM SPECIFIC IMPACTS

The switching of assembly location mid-cycle for models currently made in the UK is not likely given high "double running" costs in tooling and logistics. What is much more likely, though, is a shift of assembly at the point of model replacement or when new models are launched (LMC 2016b). Companies assessing their assembly location will consider a range of issues in making such decisions, including:

- the relative cost differences between UK and EU locations;
- the dependency of sales of the particular model on the European versus the UK market;
- the relative importance of "Made in Britain" to the brand (which is more relevant for premium and luxury brands);

5. Note, though, the attitude of the German Automotive Industry Association. A spokesperson stated: "If you want full access to the market, that comes necessarily with the free movement of people. That's the bitter pill the Brexiteers have to accept" (*AutoExpress* 2016).

- the volume of imported components;
- the location options in the EU (linked to how much capacity still exists in the European auto industry); and
- the profitability of UK operations, and how reduced free-trade conditions with the EU would affect this.

Uncertainty in particular over the possibility of tariffs places a question mark over the future of a number of UK plants and jobs. Furthermore, as supply chain investment moves with assemblers' volumes, there could be a broader knock-on effect. It should also be noted that automotive technology is changing rapidly with developments in electric cars, connected cars and autonomous (driverless) cars. As LMC (2016a) note, a lack of FDI in such new technologies could have "a long term impact on the competitiveness of the UK industry."

A major risk facing UK auto is that investment decisions for the launch of new vehicle models are made several years in advance, often with plants engaged in "locational tournaments" to win contracts to build the new models. For many companies those decisions are set to be made in the middle of Brexit negotiations which are anticipated to last two years (i.e. Article 50 activated by April 2017 with a two year negotiation). As LMC (2016b) notes, "new investment initiatives in the UK, such as expansion of current manufacturing activity, or new capacity for manufacturers that have alternatives to the UK appear unlikely until current uncertainty diminishes. Such uncertainty has the potential to last for several years."

As Table 4.1 shows, investment decisions are already likely to have been made for the production of new car models in 2017–19, including the Nissan Leaf and Juke and the Toyota Auris. However, the investment decisions for most cars which will be manufactured after 2019 are yet to be made. These include future generations of the Honda Civic, which will begin production in 2023, and future generations of the Toyota Auris and Range Rover Sport.

Those investment decisions will be made in what looks to be at least a two-year window of uncertainty. Car makers will ask: will UK auto have access to the single market? Is investing in UK production worth the risk? This risk is greater for "mass market" producers, who operate on low margins and low capacity, are reliant on exports, and have new models at the planning stage. This is why PA Consulting (2016) sees Toyota and Honda plants as at the most risk – although LMC (2016b) sees the Vauxhall Ellesmere Port plant as most at risk (for example given the high degree of imported components).

A potential withdrawal of investment was raised by Nissan and by Ford in relation to engine assembly, and the Japanese government has raised concerns over the Brexit process and how this could impact on Japanese investment

Table 4.1 Factory location choices.

Manufacturer	2017	2018	2019	2020	2021	2022	2023	2024
Honda	*Civic*						<u>Civic</u>	
Vauxhall					<u>Astra</u>		<u>MPV</u>	
Mini		*Country-man*				<u>Clubman</u>	<u>Mini</u>	
Toyota		*Auris* *Avensis*				Auris		
Nissan	*Leaf* *Juke*	*Note*		<u>Qashqai, XTrail</u>	<u>Infinity Q30</u>			
Jaguar	*XJ*				<u>F-Type</u>	<u>XF/XE</u>	<u>F-Pace</u>	<u>XJ/XJR</u>
Land Rover		*Evoque*	*New Defender*	<u>Range Rover Sport</u>		<u>Discovery Sport</u>		<u>Evoque Discovery</u>

Italics indicate the choice of factory has probably been made. Underline indicates the choice of factory is yet to be made.

Source: adapted from PA Consulting (2016).

in the UK (Government of Japan 2016). The Japanese government's memorandum has emphasized the need for the UK to retain maximum contact with the single market and maintain free movement of workers between the UK and EU. The Japanese ambassador to the UK has warned that Japanese firms could disinvest from the UK if Brexit meant that they could not make sufficient profits (Mason & Wintour 2016).

Nissan itself initially stated that it would defer decisions on where to build new generations of models currently assembled at its Sunderland plant, with the Renault-Nissan CEO Carlos Ghosn stating "important investment decisions will not be made in the dark" (*Financial Times* 2016b). It was thought that the firm was going to make the Qashqai and XTrail model decisions in early 2017 but appeared to have pulled forward the decisions to maximize leverage on the UK government in the wake of the Brexit vote and uncertainty over the future of the UK's trading relationship with the EU. The British government knew that it couldn't afford to lose the Qashqai investment and Nissan effectively held a big gun to its head. A deal was done and Nissan announced that it would build the next generation Qashqai and XTrail at Sunderland after having received "assurances" from the UK government.

The government has remained tight-lipped on what support was offered, even declining to answer requests from the Office for Budget Responsibility as to whether any contingent liabilities arise from the deal (Farrell 2016). The Qashqai decision was clearly good news for the industry and reflected the underlying competitiveness of the Sunderland plant. Yet Nissan has since said it will re-examine its investment strategy once the terms of Brexit become clear, and more broadly the bigger battles in securing investment in UK auto lie ahead – at Honda, Toyota and Vauxhall – all of which are more at risk of switching production if uncertainty over the UK's trading relationship with Europe is not clarified sooner rather than later.

While firms like Nissan will certainly face challenges if UK auto does not have access to the single market, manufacturers may also try to use uncertainty as an excuse to cut capacity in the UK as part of wider efforts to reduce over-capacity in Europe (especially so given how easy it is to lay off workers in the UK compared with other EU countries). Ford has already scaled back investment at its Bridgend engine plant, although it has denied this is linked with Brexit.

It should be noted that the UK auto industry's success rests in large part on its productivity. The UK auto industry boasts plant utilization running at over 70 per cent, with several plants running 24/7 operations (KPMG 2014). This compares favourably to European nations such as Italy, where utilization runs at just over 50 per cent. For example, Nissan's Sunderland car plant was the UK's most productive in 2015, building one-in-three of all new vehicles in the UK. The risk is that some firms will try to take advantage of spare capacity on the continent, shifting production from the UK at the time of new model launches, especially if uncertainty can be used to justify it. While some commentators such as LMC (2106b) note that while a "Hard Brexit"(here meaning exiting the single market) may not represent a severe blow to UK auto, some volume (and by implication jobs in assembly and the supply chain) is likely to be lost over the medium to long term.[6]

OTHER IMPACTS

Even with a trade deal, there is one area where UK auto will definitely lose out, and that is via the ability to influence regulation in the industry. Regulation is not going away and if anything will become more important as we move towards connected and autonomous cars. The UK will have no influence on shaping those regulations in Europe when it leaves. Jaguar Land Rover, for example, will have to look to the Slovakian government to represent it at the European level when the UK does exit (given that it is investing in an assembly plant in Slovakia).

---

6. Dhingra *et al.* (2016), drawing on Head and Mayer (2015), suggest that if the UK were not able to maintain tariff-free access to the EU, UK auto output could fall by 12 per cent if the wake of Brexit, with production shifted to elsewhere in the EU and possibly other locations.

A second possible impact centres on the availability of skilled workers. The auto industry currently has some 5,000 vacancies and needs to be able to hire skilled workers from Europe (SMMT 2016a). Again, this needs to be sorted out as quickly as possible. The extent to which automotive firms in the UK are affected by controls on immigration will, of course, depend on the nature of any new rules. One option could be to extend current rules for non-EU/EEA nationals to all non-UK nationals (House of Commons Library 2016). This would effectively restrict economic migration to highly skilled migrants, reducing the inflow of migrant workers doing low-skilled jobs. However, as noted by the Social Market Foundation (Broughton *et al.* 2016), only 12 per cent of current EEA employees working in the UK as a whole would meet visa requirements that currently apply to non-EEA workers. This might lead to labour shortages in those sectors which employ a higher share of EU migrants in their workforce, including manufacturing (at 10%) (House of Commons Library 2016). A more restrictive immigration system might also increase burdens on automotive firms if they have to spend time and resources on obtaining visas and complying with more detailed immigration regulations.

A third impact relates to university and industry access to European research funding, such as through Horizon 2020 (H2020). This is relevant as tens of millions of pounds of H2020 funding has gone to UK-based automotive firms to develop new technologies. While the Chancellor has "guaranteed" to plug science funding gaps arising from Brexit, it is not clear what this means in practice and whether British universities and firms (including in the auto industry) will be able to participate in, and benefit from, Horizon 2020 collaborative research networks in the future. Ideally what UK auto needs to see is continued British participation in Horizon 2020 and the key research networks and collaboration that this involves. That could in turn underpin private sector investment in new technologies in the sector. A final uncertainty here is over the role of the European Investment Bank which has made substantial support available to car firms in the UK to develop low carbon technologies such as more fuel efficient engines. With the UK leaving the EU, will such types of support still be forthcoming? That in turn brings us to the issue of industrial policy to which we turn below.

All of this suggests that a number of key priorities need to be spelled out as soon as possible in the UK's Brexit negotiating position so as to underpin investors' confidence in UK auto (and broader manufacturing). First, access to the single market needs to be in place for the sector. As the EEF (2016) notes, the UK must be prepared to make a contribution to the EU in order to achieve this. Second, maintaining the skills base is critical – this includes enabling UK auto to hire skilled workers from Europe. Third, and linked to the first point, regulatory cooperation with the EU needs to be ensured. Finally, measures need to be taken to underpin investment in the UK, boost productivity and to develop an effective industrial strategy (on the latter see Bailey *et al.* 2015).

INDUSTRIAL POLICY NEEDS

Britain needs to more than just strike a new trade deal with the EU. For example, British government will need to do much more to create and develop its own skills; this means developing better systems for education, skills training, and retraining as part of a wider industrial policy. Just as the government and Bank of England have had to rethink fiscal and monetary policy, so too industrial policy needs to be re-examined. Given the recent depreciation in sterling, there is potentially a new opportunity here for reshoring the auto supply chain further. That is not going to happen automatically, though, given the barriers to reshoring that have been identified (e.g. access to finance, skills, availability of land, energy costs; Bailey & De Propris 2014).

The new government under Theresa May has brought with it a marked and welcome change of tone on industrial strategy, unveiling a Green Paper and consultation in early 2017 (HM Government 2017) and emphasizing its role in the economy. But what might it mean? A quick recap of where we are may be useful. The coalition government's record in relation to industrial strategy was mixed at best. Chancellor George Osborne made promising noises in a number of budgets and autumn statements over 2010–15 about rebalancing the economy and a "march of the makers", but little was delivered in reality. Some support was made available to rebuilding the UK's fractured supply chains and to encouraging "rebalancing" but the sums on offer were small and failed to match the scale of the rhetoric. Indeed, the manufacturing recovery since the financial crisis has been weak, characterized by concerns over its durability centred on fragility in key export markets, low levels of investment spending, concerns over the impact of high energy costs across the sector, and issues of skills and access to finance down the supply chain.

The previous government did away with the old regional development authorities and replaced them with the local enterprise partnerships (LEPs). The intention of devolving more power to ground level was laudable, but in practice many powers were initially recentralized and LEPs had insufficient funding anyway. Their performance has been very mixed. While LEPs in Birmingham and the Black Country have received praise, further afield there is a question mark as to how much LEPs are really doing. In particular, they lack the regional scale to support wider development. In addition, the coalition government was slow to address the problems that small businesses face in raising finance, largely because the banks are now much more risk-averse. These companies are crucial to industrial supply chains, and this is an area that still requires attention. Recent governments have also made no attempt to address the UK's lax takeover rules, which do little to protect strategically important businesses from foreign predators, in contrast with approaches taken in some other countries.

On the positive side, the Cameron government did introduce a series of so-called "catapults". These are centres where businesses, engineers and scientists work together on late-stage research and development. The different catapults are each dedicated to different priority areas such as high-value manufacturing, transport systems and offshore renewables. They are about long-term sector development, so it is still too early to judge them, but they look like the right sort of intervention.

Equally encouraging has been the work of the Automotive Council, which started at the end of the last Labour administration and which developed under Vince Cable, the business secretary, into an effective body in fostering public–private cooperation and other initiatives. The Council's work has, for example, set out clear priorities for key automotive technologies that need to be developed (such as on powertrains, lightweighting and intelligent mobility) which has both aligned government support and funding and has underpinned business confidence and investment.

More recently, though, Sajid Javid's tenure as business secretary was disappointing. His immediate decision to sell off a majority stake in the Green Investment Bank raised questions about the government's commitment to the low carbon economy. The Automotive Council has continued. Critically, though, its work was previously backed up by a range of (modest) interventions to boost skills, rebuild supply chains, and encourage investment in the industry, such as through the Regional Growth Fund, the Advanced Manufacturing Supply Chain Initiative, the Manufacturing Advisory Service (MAS), and MAS's tooling-up fund to support investment in tools in the supply chain. All were scrapped by Javid during his time as business secretary. This was a regrettable, as where policy was reasonably well developed, as in the automotive industry, it really did make a difference. For example, interventions like the Advanced Manufacturing Supply Chain Initiative and Tooling Up Fund cost small amounts of money in the big scheme of things (£245 million and £12 million respectively).

Enter, post Brexit vote, the new business secretary, Greg Clark. What is to be done? First, the government needs to look again at LEPs and return to development bodies that can intervene more widely and strategically at a regional level, and do "smart specialization" through regional level industrial policies. Combined authorities may be one way to do that (in cities at least), and are an area where Clark has much expertise. Beefing up the local growth hubs to fill the vacuum left by the abolition of MAS could be part of this "Combined Authority Plus" model, as would complete devolution of skills funding to the regional level. Second, there is much more that the government could be doing in really trying to "rebalance" the economy and reduce Brexit-induced uncertainty, for example by stimulating investment in manufacturing such as through enhanced capital allowances, by resurrecting something like the Advanced Manufacturing Supply Chain Initiative (preferably on a much wider scale), and by plugging funding gaps for small firms in the supply chain. Third, the government should also do something about UK takeover rules to put the country on a level playing field with many of its main competitors.

Returning to the "Nissan deal", what exactly did the government offer Nissan and what does it tell us about the government's new industrial strategy and more broadly its negotiating stance on Brexit? On this we have learned a little from Greg Clark last November (Wintour 2016). Clark made it clear that a key UK objective in Brexit talks will be to avoid tariff barriers with the EU. He also made repeated reference to industry sectors and their different needs, implying that the UK would seek to negotiate sector-by-sector deals with the EU. That could see the UK trying to avoid non-tariff barriers in certain sectors like auto, effectively giving those sectors something like access to the single market. This suggests that the Business department at least sees access for sectors like auto to the EU single market as a key negotiating objective (whether the International Trade Secretary Liam Fox agrees with that is another matter, of course).

Clark's comments raised a number of points on which the government has been vague so far. First, Clark seemed to imply that – as a minimum – UK auto could remain in a customs union arrangement with the EU. That would go a long way to reassuring the auto industry on tariffs. Second, if the UK really does want to trade without tariffs and non-tariff barriers, then the EU may well extract a "price" in the form of a contribution to the EU budget, as made by Norway and Switzerland and noted above. Third, some form of "referee" may be needed to determine whether the UK is playing by the rules of whatever trade deal is done with the EU. That might be the WTO or a body linked to the EU. Fourth, despite Nissan wanting "compensation" if tariffs are imposed, Clark appeared to suggest that may not be possible under WTO rules. Finally, the government appears to have reiterated its support to the auto industry through the industrial strategy it is now developing, on issues like skills, innovation and reshoring the supply chain. The latter is welcome, and is something of a major U-turn as compared with the reign of the previous business secretary Sajid Javid.

More broadly, however, there is a strong case for UK industrial strategy to be afforded an institutional status similar to both UK monetary and fiscal policies. At the very least, it should be the subject of regular strategic long-term reviews. By giving it that sort of priority, the new government would send out the kind of powerful message that British industry and foreign investors need to hear. On a positive note, the new business secretary is perhaps unique in government in bringing with him a welcome devolving instinct (witness his efforts at "city deals") that offers the possibility to join up sectoral policy at the national level with place based policy at the regional level. However, let's hope the new government really is more serious about the need to rebalance the economy than the last one. More rhetoric about the "march of the makers" won't be enough.

CONCLUSIONS

The UK's automotive sector has been successful in recent years in growing output and – to a more limited degree – in sourcing more components locally. Brexit brings both opportunities and challenges to the industry and it is important that these are tackled effectively so that the industry can continue to thrive. The Brexit vote, for example, leaves considerable uncertainty over the nature of the UK's trading relationship with the EU. That uncertainty has the potential to impact on foreign investment in the UK auto sector, especially when auto firms are looking to replace models. While Nissan has made a (tentative) decision to build the next generation Qashqai and XTrail models at Sunderland, other firms may hold off making decisions on assembly in the UK until they know whether they will face tariffs when exporting to the EU. Plants and jobs could be at risk if such uncertainty isn't "nailed down" quickly in the form of clear parameters for a trade deal – and preferably one that is as close as possible to existing single market arrangements for the sector. On this there is much more that the government could be doing in really trying to counter this uncertainty, for example by prioritizing as part of the Brexit negotiations access to the single market for the sector and ensuring that UK firms can hire skilled workers from Europe.

The UK also needs to do more than agree a new trading relationship with Europe. It needs a new industrial strategy both to offset Brexit induced uncertainty and to "rebalance" the economy, for example by stimulating investment in manufacturing such as through enhanced capital allowances, by resurrecting something like the Advanced Manufacturing Supply Chain Initiative (preferably on a much wider scale), and by plugging funding gaps for small firms in the supply chain. There is the opportunity to "reshore" more of the auto components industry if sterling settles down at a new, lower exchange rate. That is not going to happen automatically, though, given the barriers to reshoring noted above, and an effective industrial strategy is required to push this along. It should also be noted that the industry is undergoing profound changes, with shifts towards electrification, and connected and autonomous (driverless) cars. A committed industrial strategy will be needed to underpin private sector investment in such technologies, a point which Jaguar Land Rover has been keen to stress regarding its aspiration to build electric vehicles in the UK (Bailey 2016). On this we await more details from the government's new industrial strategy. More broadly, there is a strong case for UK industrial strategy to be afforded an institutional status similar to both UK monetary and fiscal policies. At the very least, it should be the subject of regular strategic long-term reviews. By giving it that sort of priority, the new government would send out the kind of powerful message that British industry and foreign investors need to hear. The key point is that given both opportunities and risks arising from Brexit for UK auto, a better-funded and more active industrial strategy is now needed to support UK auto and manufacturing.

ACKNOWLEDGEMENTS

The writing of this chapter has in part been supported by the EU Horizon 2020 project MAKERS: Smart Manufacturing for EU Growth and Prosperity, a project funded by the Horizon 2020 Research and Innovation Staff Exchange Programme, under the Marie Sklodowska-Curie Actions, grant agreement number 691192.

REFERENCES

AutoExpress 2016. "Brexit Spells Uncertainty for UK Car Industry". *AutoExpress* (28 June). Retrieved from www.autoexpress.co.uk/car-news/consumer-news/96091/brexit-spells-uncertainty-for-uk-car-industry (accessed 29 December 2016).

Bailey, D. 2016. "JLR Throws Down the Gauntlet to Government". *Birmingham Post* (29 November). Retrieved from www.birminghampost.co.uk/business/business-opinion/jlr-throws-down-gauntlet-government-12246652 (accessed 12 January 2017).

Bailey, D. & L. De Propris 2014. "Manufacturing Reshoring and its Limits: The UK Automotive Case". *Cambridge Journal of Regions, Economy and Society* **7**(3): 379–98.

Bailey, D. & A. de Ruyter 2015. "Plant Closures, Precariousness and Policy Responses: Revisiting MG Rover Ten Years On". *Policy Studies* **36**(4): 363–83.

Bailey, D. & N. Berkeley 2014. "Regional Responses to Recession: A Case Study of the West Midlands". *Regional Studies* **48**(11): 1797–812.

Bailey, D., P. Tomlinson & K. Cowling 2015. *New Perspectives on Industrial Policy for a Modern Britain*. Oxford: Oxford University Press.

Broughton, N., N. Keohane & T. Ketola 2016. *Working Together? The Impact of the EU Referendum on UK Employers*. London: Social Market Foundation.

Coe, N. M. & H. W. Yeung 2015. *Global Production Networks*. Oxford: Oxford University Press.

Dhingra, S., G. Ottaviano, T. Sampson & J. Van Reenen 2016. *The Impact of Brexit on Foreign Investment in the UK*. CEP Brexit Analysis 3. London: LSE Centre for Economic Performance.

Driffield, N. & M. Karoglou 2016. "Brexit and Foreign Investment in the UK". Social Science Research Network. Retrieved from http://papers.ssrn.com/sol3/papers.cfm?abstract_id=2775954 (accessed 29 December 2016).

EEF 2016. *Britain and the EU: Manufacturing an Orderly Exit*. London: EEF.

Farrell, S. 2016. "Nissan in UK: Treasury Refuses to Tell OBR if Cost Attached to Decision". *The Guardian* (23 November). Retrieved from www.theguardian.com/business/2016/nov/23/nissan-in-uk-treasury-refuses-to-tell-obr-if-cost-attached (accessed 29 December 2016).

Financial Times 2016a. "UK Inflation Approaches 2-year High". *Financial Times* (16 August). Retrieved from www.ft.com/content/8d8b7338-638b-11e6-a08a-c7ac04ef00aa (accessed 29 December 2016).

Financial Times 2016b. "Nissan Delays Sunderland Investment Decisions". *Financial Times* (29 September). Retrieved from www.ft.com/content/53bc5cec-8660-11e6-a29c-6e7d9515ad15 (accessed 29 December 2016).

Gereffi, G., J. Humphrey & T. Sturgeon 2005. "The Governance of Global Value Chains". *Review of International Political Economy* **12**(1): 78–104.

Government of Japan 2016. *Japan's Message to the United Kingdom and the European Union*. Tokyo: Government of Japan. Retrieved from www.mofa.go.jp/files/000185466.pdf (accessed 29 December 2016).

HM Government 2017. *Building Our Industrial Strategy*. Green Paper. London: HM Government.

Head, K. & T. Mayer 2015. *Brands in Motion: How Frictions Shape Multinational Production*. UBC working paper. Paris: CEPII. Retrieved from www.cepii.fr/PDF_PUB/wp/2015/wp2015-26.pdf (accessed 29 December 2016).

Holmes, P. 2016. "A Special Deal for the Car Industry: How Could it Work?" Retrieved from www.sussex.ac.uk/eu/articles/brexit-special-deal (accessed 29 December 2016).

House of Commons Library 2016. "Brexit: Impact Across Policy Areas". Briefing Paper 07213. Retrieved from http://researchbriefings.parliament.uk/ResearchBriefing/Summary/CBP-7213#fullreport (accessed 29 December 2016).

KPMG 2014. *The UK Automotive Industry and the EU*. London: KPMG.

KPMG 2016. *Brexit: How Would Business Vote?* London: KPMG.

LMC 2016a. *Client Alert: Implications of UK Vote to leave the European Union*. London: LMC Automotive.

LMC 2016b. *Client Alert: Brexit Analysis Update: UK Vehicle Industry Risk; and What if Things get Worse?* London: LMC Automotive.

Mason, R. & P. Wintour 2016. "Japanese Ambassador Warns Companies Could Leave UK over Brexit". *The Guardian* (5 September). Retrieved from www.theguardian.com/politics/2016/sep/05/japanese-ambassador-warns-companies-could-leave-uk-over-brexit (accessed 29 December 2016).

Mathews, J. A. 2006. "Dragon Multinationals: New Players in 21st Century Globalization". *Asia Pacific Journal of Management* **23**(1): 5–27.

PA Consulting 2016. *Brexit: The Impact on Automotive Manufacturing in the UK.* London: PA Consulting.

SMMT 2016a. *2016 Sustainability Report.* London: Society of Motor Traders and Manufacturers.

SMMT 2016b. "SMMT 100th Annual Dinner Speech by Gareth Jones, SMMT President". London: Society of Motor Traders and Manufacturers. Retrieved from www.smmt.co.uk/2016/11/society-of-motor-manufacturers-and-traders-100th-annual-dinner-speech-gareth-jones-smmt-president (accessed 12 January 2017).

Wintour, P. 2016. "Greg Clark's Big Reveal on 'Demeanour' of Brexit Negotiations Strategy". *The Guardian* (30 November). Retrieved from www.theguardian.com/politics/2016/oct/30/greg-clark-brexit-negotiations-andrew-marr-show-nissan-auto-industry (accessed 29 December 2016).

CHAPTER 5

FUTURE REGULATION OF THE UK WORKFORCE

Sukhwinder Salh, Margarita Nyfoudi and Alex de Ruyter

INTRODUCTION

This chapter examines the scenarios facing the UK workforce given the "Brexit" referendum vote on 23 June 2016 which resulted in a vote to leave the EU. Focusing on freedom of movement and the European Working Time Directive, the chapter considers the regulation of the employment relationship and what the impact of Brexit on this could be. We argue that the overall effect on the UK workforce will largely be dictated by what type of trading relationship the UK is able to obtain with the EU and the rest of the world. If the UK wishes to retain access to the single market then it will probably have to accept continued freedom of movement and abiding by the EU social chapter of workers' rights. However, if it wishes to restrict freedom of movement, as public statements to date by the UK government have indicated, then a more limited relationship with the EU would most likely ensue, but potentially allow the UK government more room to make changes to regulating the employment relationship. Attempts to restrict freedom of movement could also have wider implications for sectors of the UK economy reliant on EU migrant workers or those that export into the EU.

THE EU AND THE REGULATION OF EMPLOYMENT

During the referendum campaign, one of the key themes articulated by Remain campaigners was that a vote to leave the EU was a vote to drastically alter (i.e. reduce) the scope of protective employment regulations in the UK workplace. In response to this, the Leave campaign argued that freedom of movement and consequent migration of workers from Central and Eastern European member states was depriving British workers of jobs (and access to school places, doctors' appointments and social services) and was lowering wages in the economy. A vote for Leave was a vote to "take back control" of the UK border and reduce immigration. That the vote for Leave was significant in the traditional Labour-voting areas of the old industrial Midlands, north of England and Welsh valleys suggests that arguments around migration and low-paid workers had more traction with voters than any nascent concerns over employment rights.[1] Research for the Joseph Rowntree Foundation (Goodwin & Heath 2016) suggested that workers on low incomes were more likely to support Brexit.

That much work in the UK is low-paid and insecure, with analysis by John Philpott suggesting that over 7 million workers, or some 22.2 per cent of the workforce in 2016 (up from 18.1% in 2006) were in precarious forms of employment (Booth 2016),[2] only further served to reinforce perceptions that for those caught in precarious work, the platform of employment rights were already minimal (if indeed enforced). This is in a context whereby the average wage for *full-time* employees (that is, *median* average salary for the tax year ending 5 April 2015) was only £27,600 (Income Tax Calculator 2016). Recent high-profile cases reported in the media against companies such as Uber, Deliveroo and Sports Direct have served to illustrate the conditions facing such precarious workers. Uber, for example, recently lost a court case brought against it by a number of its own drivers. The judges in this case upheld the drivers' claims that they should be treated as employees (rather than "self-employed") and hence receive a statutory national minimum wage, holiday pay and sick pay (Booth 2016). Therefore, there was little "left to lose" for such voters by voting to leave an EU that was purportedly captured by elite "metropolitan" agendas (Pidd 2016).

It is against this backdrop, then, that the impact of the EU on the current body of UK employment regulations needs to be considered. Developments in UK labour law over the period of EU membership (1973–present) have been shaped by two key agendas. The first of these was the Thatcherite agenda of shifting regulation to a more market-oriented stance (somewhat

---

1. This was despite there being a lack of any credible evidence to link migration to increased inequality, rather than say increased options for transnational capital during this period, as driving rising inequality (Onaran & Guschanski 2016).
2. Precarious employment here is defined as those who could lose their job at "short or no notice". Of the 22.2% of the workforce defined as such in 2016, 15.1% of the workforce were "self-employed", 4.3% on a temporary contract, and 2.9% on "zero hours" contracts (which only comprised 0.5% of the workforce in 2006). Of the self-employed category, Philpott's analysis for the Resolution Foundation suggests that half are low paid and "take home less than two-thirds of the median earnings" and that 2 million self-employed workers were earning less than £8 per hour (Booth 2016).

misleadingly labelled as "deregulation") during the 1980s and 1990s (Standing 1997). However, the second period, coinciding largely with the period of the last Labour government (1997–2010) was one of increasing prominence of statutory regulation of the employment relationship, driven by the adoption of EU directives; most notably on working-time, but also equal rights for part-time and temporary employees, information and consultation rights in the workplace, and various other provisions encapsulated in the Maastricht Social Chapter (Waring *et al.* 2006). In this sense, the UK industrial relations system could be seen to have shifted from one of voluntaristic collective bargaining with little direct state involvement other than setting minimum wages and conditions in residual sectors, to an individualist set-up underpinned by a platform of statutory employment rights.

The more recent period of Conservative–Liberal Democrat (2010–15) and now Conservative government (2015–present) has to date seen a limited rollback of protective legislation, notably around statutory service thresholds for unfair dismissal law and trade union rights which were not covered under EU provisions (Heyes 2016). However, this is only to emphasize the point that as an EU member state, the UK government has been largely bound by the social policy provisions attached to membership of the single market. In this context, previous Conservative election manifesto statements have emphasized repatriation of employment powers from the EU. In the lead-up to negotiations over the UK's continued membership of the EU, it was expected that the then prime minister, David Cameron, would demand repatriation of powers relating to the European Working Time Directive (EWTD) and Temporary Agency Workers Directive. However, these were not pursued as they would have necessitated major treaty revisions (*ibid.*). Still, as Heyes notes, that these would be flagged as items for negotiation points to the continued "genuine desire of many Conservative politicians to end EU influence over UK employment legislation" (*ibid.*).

It is here, then, that the crux of the issue is reached – EU public figures such as Jean-Claude Juncker, chairman of the EU Commission, have insisted that freedom of movement and adherence to EU social provisions must be upheld if the UK wishes to retain access to the single market. In contrast, public statements to date from the UK prime minister, Theresa May, and other senior figures within her government, have stipulated that "control of borders" and hence restrictions on freedom of movement, must be paramount (Booth 2016). However, the UK government has not yet expressed any firm stance on the thrust of employment regulation. This in itself should not be surprising, as the slant of any future developments in this regard will be determined by the nature of the relationship with the EU that is ultimately negotiated. In a similar fashion, trading relationships with the rest of the world (particularly in the form of bilateral trade treaties, as the contentious debate around TTIP, the proposed US–EU Transatlantic Trade and Investment Partnership, attests; see Monbiot 2013) will also affect the direction of travel of employment law legislation.

Changes to domestic UK legislation such as increasing the qualifying period of unfair dismissal, indicates a government with an appetite to assist in the management of the employment relationship. With the aim of encouraging more autonomy and handing back control to employers, this enables disputes to be determined at a local level as opposed to going to employment tribunals. This theme of "control" has been used by Leave campaigners, who have employed this tactic and the notion of claiming back sovereignty as part of their overall strategy, which has clearly paid dividends as this rhetoric continues to percolate through political speeches and discourse. Since the Brexit vote confirmed the UK's departure from the EU, questions have begun to emerge about what regulations will be amended or repealed. Until the current government confirms the exact exit strategy to be adopted, we can only really speculate about the challenges in the future. A closer examination of the UK government's approach in the past and of the examples of legal intervention given earlier could give some indication of how the current government proposes to deal with EU regulations post-Brexit. Attempting to examine the full range of regulations that impact on the UK labour market is an ambitious exercise. However, by focusing on one or two individual aspects of EU legal regulation we can explore some of the possible issues that will face UK workplaces. In the material that follows, we focus on two case studies – freedom of movement and the EWTD – in order to gain a deeper understanding of the particular work and employment issues that Brexit is likely to entail.

THE EUROPEAN WORKING TIME DIRECTIVE

The European Working Time Directive (EWTD) was formally implemented in the UK on 1 October 1998 by the then Labour government. Uncertainty after the Brexit vote has questioned whether the EWTD will still apply in its current format. Although known for outlining the limit on a working week, which should not exceed 48 hours (over an average 17-week period), this is not the only impact of the directive. The remit of the EWTD is much wider and includes the right to paid annual leave, rest periods, rules for night workers and the definition of "on call". Hence the scope of the EWTD is wide and application of the rules has resulted in conflicting views from EU and the UK government, which makes this regulation a strong contender for change.

A controversial aspect of the rules on the working week was the opt-out, under which the 48-hour limit does not apply if a worker signs a written agreement to that effect with the employer (Davies 2015). This provision of the opt-out was negotiated by the UK government in order to gain a degree of flexibility in the way in which businesses could operate and allowed them to avoid the 48-hour working week rule. Critics of the opt-out argue that it is inconsistent to have such a provision as it moves away from the original rationale for the EWTD, which is to ensure health and safety in the work-place. Going forward it will be interesting to see if this desire for flexibility will be pushed further post-Brexit. History would suggest this is an area to watch. The Conservative government unwillingly agreed to the EWTD: in November 1993 negotiations over the implementation of the EWTD between member states and the UK government failed, and the UK government was outvoted by eleven to one (Analytica Daily Brief 2016). The Conservatives strongly opposed the directive because it went against their neoliberal agenda that gave primacy to market forces, and was an affront both to the right of employers and to individual liberty and choice (Gall 2011).

This historical context would suggest that this is exactly the type of EU directive that the UK government will revisit, given employers' particular dis-dain for European Court of Justice (ECJ) rulings that have consistently upheld EU directives. Further support for the view that employers are increasingly becoming vocal about the difficulties of these rulings is confirmed in a BIS analysis paper (Devlin & Shirvani 2014). An example of rulings that have been shown to be problematic for the UK labour market can be seen in the recent appeal judgement of the case *British Gas Trading* v. *Lock* (2016), which centres on the issue of holiday pay calculations. First heard by the ECJ back in March 2014; later that year it was confirmed by an employment tribunal that a worker must be paid in respect of periods of annual leave by reference to commission payments in order to comply with European law. A further appeal by the employers was instigated and the appeal judgement in 2016 reconfirms a requirement to comply with previous ECJ rulings. A large num-ber of claims were "stayed" pending the outcome of this decision, and it was reported British Gas has around 1,000 potential claims from its workers wait-ing in the wings (Simpson 2015). In the absence of clear direction from the government about which EU regulations may be subject to change it leaves British Gas to consider the only other available option of a further appeal to the Supreme Court.

The argument of giving workers autonomy and the option to work longer hours in order to make ends meet is just one view. The opposing argument is simply that the dilution of the EWTD could create an environment of exploitation and oppression, which in itself can impact on morale and productivity for businesses as well as placing workers at risk in terms of health and safety. If a post-Brexit government moves forward by deregulating the UK labour market as much as possible, or at least modify existing policy in the name of flexibility, this could imply a future outside the single market, which could imply a "bonfire" of regulations (Coulter & Hancke 2016). How employers respond to ensuring the preservation of the work–life balance that the EWTD aims to promote will be a key factor for the UK government to consider.

Turning to holiday leave, employment rights relating to holiday pay have been an increasing area of conflict and a range of ECJ rulings have continued to add to the confusion. A continual flow of case law has prompted the need for clarity as decisions on how holiday pay should be calculated and what elements of remuneration should be included when on annual leave have been highly controversial. The issues most commonly cited by business groups in relation to the EWTD generally do not relate to the core provisions of the directive, but instead focus on the impacts of rulings made by the EU after the directive was adopted. These appear to have increased employer costs significantly, with the possibility of more impact from the most recent judgments around holiday pay (Devlin & Shirvani 2014). Reviewing some of the leading decisions can provide further insight on the impact of the EU on the workplace and the degree of ambiguity this has presented. The *Williams* v. *British Airways plc* (2011) case concerned airline pilots' pay and the ECJ ruled that pilots were entitled to be paid their normal remuneration during their four week period of statutory annual leave. Holiday pay must include all elements of remuneration, such as flying pay supplements, and not just basic pay (Davies 2015). The consequences from an employer's perspective are that the cost of managing such payments immediately increases, and could even prompt businesses to review the additional payments, commission or allowances that are offered to employees as part of their overall terms and conditions. From an EU perspective the overall goal of the EWTD is to encourage rest periods and maintain health and safety standards, hence such a stance from the EU was, in many ways, inevitable. The EU were keen to ensure employees were not deterred from taking their annual holiday because of a loss of income.

A more recent example of the complexity of the ECJ rulings and impact on the UK labour market was evident in the leading Spanish case known as *Tyco* (2015), brought by a group of technicians employed by the company and referred to the Advocate General in 2015 (Faragher 2015). The ECJ held that the journeys made by workers without a fixed or habitual place of work between their homes and the first and last customer of the day constitutes working time. This decision in *Tyco* (2015) prompted accusations against the

EU of "tormenting" businesses, as the judgment had significant implications for workers such as carers, electricians, gas fitters and anyone else who moves from job to job. The ECJ dismissed arguments by the UK that counting travel time as working time would inevitably lead to higher costs for business as travel time does not need to be paid under domestic UK law (Robinson *et al.* 2015). However, a relevant implication of this ruling is the need for employers to remain vigilant when monitoring compliance with the 48 hours per week limit.

Further problematic interpretations that have arisen from the EWTD include the definition of being "on call". Additional restrictions from the *SiMAP*[3] (2000) ruling resulted in on-call time for doctors who are on site and expected to be available to count as working time (Goddard 2016). This ruling requires those that employ staff on an on-call basis to review their work patterns and develop new internal policies. However, for the NHS the relationship with the implementation of the EWTD has been incredibly complex. Goddard (*ibid.*) argues that removing the impact of rulings such as *SiMAP* would allow for more flexibility of on-call working and could be a fruitful test case in the "brave new world" outside the EU. However, there does appear to be some support for the spirit of the EWTD, as the UK has worked hard to comply with its requirements. Elisabetta Zanon, director of the NHS European Office, argues that rather than the directive itself causing problems, it is the European Court of Justice's rulings on rest periods that can cause difficulties for employers (Rimmer 2016).

A view that reinforces concern with the ECJ rulings is shared by the CBI, which has highlighted that the implications of these rulings could leave firms open to abuse by workers (ACAS 2014). Such concerns from UK businesses led to the development of an EU business taskforce report (Business Taskforce 2013), which was commissioned by David Cameron as a result of complaints about ECJ rulings linked to EWTD. Clearly this demonstrates the experience with the implementation of the EWTD has been turbulent and an opportunity to revisit the directive is welcomed. The UK government and employers have regarded these ECJ rulings as unwelcome, given the implications of additional costs, monitoring, and flexibility required from employers. As such, it is quite possible that post-Brexit, the UK government may wish to clarify the manner in which payments during annual leave are calculated and hence provide their own definition of working time. Hence, it is likely, given the contested nature of cases covered under the EWTD that this is a key area in which the government may seek to make changes to employment

---

3. Case C-303/98, *Sindicato de Medicos de Asistencia Publica (SiMAP)* v. *Conselleria de Sanidad y consumo de la Generalidad Valenciana* (2000) ECR 1-7963.

regulation. However, the EWTD is enshrined in UK law, and hence would require an Act of Parliament to amend it – and likewise other EU statutes that have been incorporated into UK law. Given the complexities around legislative change (i.e. the volume of legislation needed) and the likely opposition of unions, including the British Medical Association, it is possible that the UK government will be unable to rush into redrafting regulations pertaining to working time (Goddard 2016).

FREEDOM OF MOVEMENT

The right of EU citizens to reside with their families and work in any member state of the Union was established in the Treaty on European Union that was signed in the Treaty of Maastricht and later amended in the Treaty on the Functioning of the European Union. The treaties and the subsequent directive 2004/38/EC and Regulations (EU) no. 492/201 and (EC) no. 883/2004 stipulate that EU workers should not be discriminated against on the basis of their nationality for employment, remuneration and social security. In other words, EU citizens do not require visas in order to seek employment in the UK and vice versa, British nationals may freely reside and work in any member state of the EU.

Should the UK wish to maintain access to the EU single market (perhaps even for certain sectors) then, as noted, it appears all but certain that the EU will demand continued guarantees of freedom of movement of EU workers as a necessary condition. In this context then, if free movement of labour is not abolished, EU citizens and British nationals would continue to enjoy their current rights in the UK and the rest of the EU member states respectively. Yet such a scenario is unlikely to take place (given the centrality of this issue to the Leave campaign, which secured 51.9% of the vote), and it is speculated that a certain degree of control will be pursued. The prime minister and other key figures in her Cabinet have already made statements to this effect. As such, decisions need to be made not only for the 3.3 million EU nationals who currently reside in the UK (Wadsworth, Dhingra, Ottaviano & Van Reenen 2016) and any future EU migrants arriving to the country, but also for the 1.2 million British nationals who presently live and work in any of the 27 other EU member states (United Nations 2015).

Should the UK chooses to restrict the free movement of labour, there are three possible scenarios for EU citizens arriving in the UK to work after Brexit. The first is that some type of visa points-based system may be established. This could be the adoption of that currently existing for non-EU foreign nationals in the form of the Tier System (see Table 5.1), which requires

Table 5.1 UK tier visa system.

Tier 1	Tier 2	Tier 3	Tier 4	Tier 5
High-value migrants • Exceptional talent • Entrepreneur • Investor • General	Skilled workers • General • Minister of religion • Sportsperson • Intra-company transfer • Priority service	Low-skilled workers	Student • Child student • General student	Temporary workers • Creative and sporting • Charity worker • Religious worker • International agreement • Youth mobility scheme

Source: UK Government (www.gov.uk/browse/visas-immigration)

employer sponsorship. At current salary levels, it is highly likely that the majority of the incoming EU workers applying for Tier 2 and Tier 3 visas in the future would not be eligible unless employers were willing to cover the difference in salary. This could impact on productivity and organizational gains (especially, with regard to Tier 3 visas), while companies' access to suitably skilled workers could be severely hindered (more relevant to Tier 2 visas). Restrictions to suitably skilled and priced labour could militate against a multinational company (MNC) locating its business in the UK or contribute to a decision to relocate their operations to EU member states, where they could access a much larger pool of skilled workers with lower administrative and bureaucratic expense.[4]

Alternatively, a points-based system similar to the one established in Australia has been mooted. EU workers would not have to secure sponsorship by an employer, but meet certain requirements, including their ability to work in a listed skilled occupation. This scenario would seem to offer more advantage to UK employers seeking skilled workers (Tier 2 visas), but would still disadvantage enterprises that utilize low-skilled workers. Currently, 14 per cent of elementary jobs (such as labourers and cleaners) are filled by EU workers (UK Commission for Employment and Skills 2015) and despite the fact that only a small increase of such jobs is projected by 2022 (Irwin 2015), there is still an imminent need to replace the large portion of UK incumbents due to retire in the following years. Table 5.2 depicts the top 10 industries

---

4. In this context then, it should not be surprising that ministers are now acknowledging that this might be unfeasible (Mason 2016).

Table 5.2 Top 10 industries with the highest proportion of EEA employees.

Industry	Proportion of EEA employees
Accommodation and food services	14%
Manufacturing	10%
Agriculture, forestry and mining	10%
Admin and support services	9%
Transport and storage	9%
Information and communication	6%
Wholesale, retail and repair of services	6%
Financial, insurance and real estate	6%
Professional, scientific or technical activity	6%
Construction	5%

Source: Social Market Foundation (2016)

with the highest proportion of employees born in one of the countries of the European Economic Area (EEA).

A third, less drastic, but more customized scenario is the establishment of a scheme by which incoming EU workers would be eligible to seek work in the UK after Brexit without any restrictions, but are only allowed to enjoy access to welfare benefits and healthcare once they are under employment. Given that this was one of the main arguments of the Leave campaign (Free Movement 2016), such a scheme would satisfy the Leave voters; however, the length of time and the type of employment, under which they would need to be employed in order to be eligible to claim benefits and healthcare access, could be a difficult clause to negotiate. Certainly, from an employer's perspective, this latter scenario appears to be the least damaging, provided that EU workers could enjoy similar rights to UK nationals as soon as they start working and under any type of employment (e.g. part-time working). Yet, it is less clear whether such a policy would be beneficial, if the UK was to be denied access to the single market. Indeed, even in the latter case it is possible that several European-facing companies would consider relocating to a more EU-friendly neighbouring country, which would eventually lead to an increase in redundancies and unemployment.

While the scenarios mentioned above constitute three of the most feasible scenarios for any incoming EU workers after Brexit, should the UK government abolish the free movement of labour, it does not necessarily follow that it would choose to follow a similar policy for the 3.3 million EU citizens currently residing in the UK. Excluding self-employed and dependants, EU workers in the UK account for 1.6 million individuals or 6 per cent of the UK workforce. These individuals make a positive fiscal contribution to the UK economy (Dustmann & Frattini 2014) in that they claim less in benefits than what they pay in taxes. Furthermore, EU workers are eligible for permanent residence if they reside in the UK for five years and may apply for a British passport after six years of residency (UK Government 2016). Hence, it is likely that different provisions will be made for this segment of EU citizens.

One possible scenario is to leave unaffected all EU workers who have already acquired a permanent right to reside in the UK. For those who are not yet eligible to remain, they would be required to join the same scheme as the people arriving in the UK after Brexit (one of the possible scenarios discussed above). Yet, given that most likely there would be a certain period of grace, a lot of EU workers who are not currently eligible for permanent residence would be within that time frame. This would reduce the likelihood of discontent from current EU workers, while reassuring employers of continuation of the status quo. However, there is no guarantee that current EU workers would choose to continue to live in the UK should the economy go into recession. Indeed, there is anecdotal evidence to suggest that after the fluctuations of sterling following the referendum on 23 June 2016, a significant number of Polish immigrants decided to move back to a booming Poland. Given that Polish workers accounted for 29 per cent of EU workers in the UK in 2015, it is difficult to predict the extent to which such movements would affect skills shortages and the availability of low-cost labour. While it appears likely that a majority of EU citizens who currently work in the UK will remain unaffected, there is less certainty for those who either might not qualify for permanent residence or might not find themselves at work at the time any relevant measures occur (e.g. they are made redundant, are unemployed, or on long-term sick leave).

With regard to the 1.2 million UK nationals currently residing in one of the 27 other EU member states, there is much more uncertainty if the UK government chooses to abolish the free movement of labour, as their status depends not only on one of the above possible Brexit scenarios, but also on the stance the EU member states will adopt. In this respect, the EU member states may choose to follow a common or a *per se* immigration strategy. The first case seems more likely to happen if the UK government manages to negotiate an ad hoc type of agreement, although EU leadership has repeatedly left little room for negotiations in terms of a special UK deal (Zeffman 2016). In this case, it is highly likely the EU immigration policy towards UK nationals would mirror the UK immigration policy towards EU nationals. Alternatively, in the second case, the UK government will need to negotiate bilateral agreements with each EU member state *per se*. In this respect, it is more likely in the interest of the UK government to focus primarily on those countries with higher concentration of UK nationals (such as Spain, Ireland

and France), leaving the rest of the UK nationals living and working in the EU less protected and more insecure in terms of their residence in the short run. Table 5.3 depicts the EU member states with the highest concentration of UK nationals.

Figure 5.1 outlines the most likely scenarios in terms of Brexit and its impact on the free movement of labour. In summary, if Brexit negotiations result in restrictions to the freedom of movement for EU workers, it is highly likely that the UK labour market will experience severe challenges. Companies facing import tariffs or other increases in the costs of doing business in the UK could well relocate their operations to other EU countries. The Japanese government has already expressed concerns in this regard, and has called for clarity on the matter by the UK government. Any loss of production by MNCs in the UK then will in turn increase unemployment, which could disproportionately affect regions such as the Midlands and North of England, which are reliant on manufacturing. Restrictions on the availability of EU workers could have knock-on effects in industries reliant on low-skilled labour in the form of reduced labour supply and hence increases in the costs of production. Such sectors include the NHS, social and community care and also agriculture. In this context, it is notable that some 7 per cent of employees in the "caring, leisure and other service occupations" in 2015 were on zero hours contracts (Booth 2016).

Prima facie, any restriction on migrant workers could serve to increase wages in these sectors. However, such wage rises could also serve to drive companies out of business in these sectors. In addition, areas such as financial services, which rely on favoured status to have access to the single market

Table 5.3 Top 10 EU member states with the highest concentration of UK nationals.

EU member state	Number of UK nationals*
Spain	309,000
Ireland	255,000
France	185,000
Germany	103,000
Italy	65,000
Netherlands	50,000
Cyprus	41,000
Poland	35,000
Belgium	27,000
Sweden	25,000

* Numbers are round to the nearest 1,000.

Source: United Nations (2015)

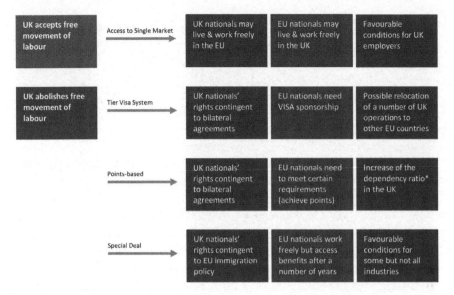

Figure 5.1 Brexit, free movement of labour and the impact on Labour: a summary of the most likely scenarios.

*Dependency ratio represents the amount of non-working, dependent citizens (e.g. pensioners, students) divided by the amount of working citizens.

could be heavily hit should the EU erect barriers to passporting rights.[5] Given the prominence of these industries to the UK economy, they have considerable lobbying ability and hence the UK government will come under severe pressure to accommodate their interests during any negotiations with the EU. For these reasons, it is reasonable to expect that there will have to be some compromise. However, it is too early to say with any certainty how the situation will pan out.

CONCLUSION

This chapter has provided a brief analysis of the possible impacts of Brexit on the UK workforce, focusing on issues relating to freedom of movement for EU workers, and the implementation of the EWTD as key areas of contention. At the time of writing the exact nature of Brexit ("soft" with single market access, or "hard", without single market access) has yet to be determined,

---

5. One estimate, provided by Oliver Wyman consultancy, suggests up to 35,000 jobs could be at risk with "hard Brexit" without access to the single market, and £5 billion in tax revenue (Treanor 2016).

so it is difficult to assess with any certainty the UK government's or the EU's intentions in this regard. However, what has become apparent through statements by the prime minister and other key figures in her government is that control of migration is a priority. With a stated deadline of 31 March 2017 to enact Article 50 of the Lisbon Treaty (the current Supreme Court hearing notwithstanding), a clearer picture should emerge quickly. In this context, the Conservative Party 2016 annual conference in Birmingham gave some insights into current thinking. There were statements from key ministers expressing that companies should disclose the number of foreign-born workers they employ, that the UK government will make it more difficult for international students to study in the UK (jeopardizing export earnings in a sector worth millions), and that foreign-born doctors should only be regarded as "interim" providers in the NHS. However, the prime minister has also made statements pointing to addressing the needs of those "just about managing", and No. 10 has also expressed concerns at the conditions of work for those in precarious forms of employment; most notably in the lack of training opportunities for those in self-employment (Booth 2016). In this context, Philip Hammond's 2016 autumn statement contained a number of measures aimed at addressing the plight of precarious low-paid workers. Among these, the most significant was an announcement of a 30 pence increase in the national minimum wage from £7.20 to £7.50 per hour (BBC 2016).

Such statements point to a highly uncertain environment for the UK workforce. As discussed, it could reasonably be expected that there might be little attempt to reduce the scope of protective employment legislation beyond the EWTD and some measures pertaining to union recognition and activity. However, attempts to control migration might lead to skills shortages in certain sectors and hence wage rises. Equally, business pressure could lead to the UK government relaxing criterion on migration in certain sectors, in the event of a "hard" Brexit. Rising inflation in the form of a devalued pound and hence higher import prices have placed additional pressures on purchasing power, which would also mitigate the impact of Chancellor Hammond's attempts at wage relief, as mentioned above. In addition, any nascent boost to export competitiveness could be undermined by increases in the cost of imported parts and components. At the time of writing, the most likely Brexit outcome looks to be some form of customs union arrangement with the EU, but exclusion from the EU single market. While this might provide a modicum of stability for the manufacturing sector in terms of no tariffs, the presence of significant non-tariff barriers to trade might yet entail significant costs to the UK economy in terms of lost foreign direct investment, higher unemployment, stagnant real wages and hence leave many people worse off. It remains to be seen how events progress.

REFERENCES

ACAS 2014. "CBI Sounds Warning about European Court Holiday Pay Ruling". Retrieved from www.acas.org.uk/index.aspx?articleid=4908 (accessed 18 January 2017).

Analytica Daily Brief 2016. "EU/UK: Institutions Bicker Over Working Time Directive". Oxford Analytica Daily Brief Service. Retrieved from https://dailybrief.oxan.com/Analysis/DB155428/EU-UK-Institutions-bicker-over-Working-Time-Directive (accessed 27 September 2016).

BBC 2016. "Autumn Statement 2016 Summary: Key Points at-a-Glance". *BBC News* (23 November). Retrieved from www.bbc.co.uk/news/uk-politics-38075649 (accessed 28 November 2016).

Booth, R. 2016. "More than 7m Britons Now in Precarious Employment". *The Guardian* (15 November). Retrieved from www.theguardian.com/uk-news/2016/nov/15/more-than-7m-britons-in-precarious-employment (accessed 18 November 2016).

Business Taskforce 2013. *Cut EU Red Tape: Report from the Business Taskforce.* London: Prime Minister's Office and Department for Business, Innovation & Skills. Retrieved from www.gov.uk/government/publications/cut-eu-red-tape-report-from-the-business-taskforce (accessed 18 January 2017).

Coulter, S. & B. Hancké 2016. "A Bonfire of the Regulations, or Business as Usual? The UK Labour Market and the Political Economy of Brexit". *Political Quarterly* **87**(2): 148–56.

Davies, A. C. L. 2015. *Employment Law.* Harlow: Pearson Education.

Devlin, C. & A. Shirvani (2014) *The Impact of the Working Time Regulations on the UK labour market: A Review of Evidence.* BIS/14/1287. London: Department for Business, Innovation and Skills. Retrieved from www.gov.uk/government/uploads/system/uploads/attachment_data/file/389676/bis-14-1287-the-impact-of-the-working-time-regulations-on-the-uk-labour-market-a-review-of-evidence.pdf (accessed 18 January 2017).

Dustmann, C. & T. Frattini 2014. "The Fiscal Effects of Immigration to the UK". *Economic Journal* **124**(FI): 593–643.

Faragher, J. 2015. "Mobile Workers' Journeys to and from Work Count as Working Time – ECJ Ruling". *Personnel Today* (September). Retrieved from www.personneltoday.com/hr/mobile-workers-journeys-work-count-working-time-ecj-ruling (accessed 18 January 2017).

Free Movement 2016. "After a Hard BREXIT: British Citizens and Residence in the EU". 9 November. Retrieved from www.freemovement.org.uk/after-a-hard-brexit-british-citizens-and-residence-in-the-eu (accessed 18 January 2017).

Gall, G. 2011. "Why Revisit the Working Time Directive?". *The Guardian* (21 November). Retrieved from www.theguardian.com/commentisfree/2011/nov/21/working-time-directive-lisbon-treaty (accessed 30 December 2016).

Goddard, A. F. 2016. "Goodbye to the European Working Time Directive?". *BMJ* **354**: i3702.

Goodwin, M. & O. Heath 2016. "Brexit Vote Explained: Poverty, Low Skills and Lack of Opportunities". Report for the Joseph Rowntree Foundation. Retrieved from www.jrf.org.uk/report/brexit-vote-explained-poverty-low-skills-and-lack-opportunities (accessed 27 September 2016).

Heyes, J. 2016. "After Brexit Where Next for UK Employment Rights?". Sheffield Political Economy Research Institute comment blog, 14 July. Retrieved from http://speri.dept.shef.ac.uk/2016/07/14/after-brexit-where-next-for-uk-employment-rights (accessed 2 September 2016).

Income Tax Calculator 2016. "Average Salary UK 2016/2017". Retrieved from www.incometaxcalculator.org.uk/average-salary-uk.php (accessed 22 November 2016).

Irwin, G. 2015. "Brexit: The Impact on the UK and the EU". London: Global Counsel. Retrieved from www.global-counsel.co.uk/sites/default/files/special-reports/downloads/Global%20Counsel_Impact_of_Brexit.pdf (accessed 12 September 2016).

Mason, R. 2016. "No 10 Rules Out Points-Based Immigration System for Britain". *The Guardian* (5 September). Retrieved from www.theguardian.com/uk-news/2016/sep/05/no-10-theresa-may-rules-out-points-based-immigration-system-for-britain-brexit (accessed 30 December 2016).

Monbiot, G. 2013. "This Transatlantic Trade Deal is a Full-Frontal Assault on Democracy". *The Guardian* (4 November). Retrieved from www.theguardian.com/commentisfree/2013/nov/04/us-trade-deal-full-frontal-assault-on-democracy (accessed 30 December 2016).

Onaran, Ö. & A. Guschanski 2016. *Rising Inequality in the UK and the Political Economy of Brexit: Lessons for Policy*. Policy Brief. London: Greenwich Political Economy Research Centre (GPERC). Retrieved from http://gala.gre.ac.uk/15630/27/15630%20ONARAN_Political_Economy_of_Brexit_2016.pdf (accessed 26 September 2016).

Pidd, H. 2016. "Blackpool's Brexit Voters Revel in 'Giving the Metropolitan Elite a Kicking'". *The Guardian* (27 June). Retrieved from www.theguardian.com/uk-news/2016/jun/27/blackpools-brexit-voters-revel-in-giving-the-metropolitan-elite-a-kicking (accessed 13 November 2016).

Rimmer, A. 2016. "What Brexit Means for the European Working Time Directive". *BMJ* **354**: i3748.

Robinson, D., A. Barker & S. Gordon 2015. "European Court of Justice accused of 'tormenting' business". *Financial Times* (10 September). Retrieved from www.ft.com/content/3482f4d0-57cc-11e5-a28b-50226830d644 (accessed 16 January 2017).

Simpson, S. 2015. "Employment Law Cases 2016: Eight Decisions to Look Out For". *Personnel Today* (15 December). Retrieved from www.personneltoday.com/hr/employment-law-cases-2016-decisions-to-look-out-for (accessed 18 January 2017).

Social Market Foundation 2016. "Working Together? The Impact of the EU Referendum on UK Employers". Retrieved from www.smf.co.uk/publications/working-together-the-impact-of-the-eu-referendum-on-uk-employers (accessed 26 September 2016).

Standing, G. 1997. "Globalization, Labour Flexibility and Insecurity: The Era of Market Regulation". *European Journal of Industrial Relations* **3**(1): 7–37.

Treanor, J. 2016. "How Are Businesses Responding to Theresa May's Proposals?". *The Guardian* (5 October). Retrieved from www.theguardian.com/politics/2016/oct/05/theresa-may-business-proposals-foreign-workers-tory (accessed 5 October 2016).

UK Commission for Employment and Skills 2015. "UKCES Labour Market Projections for the UK: 2012 to 2022". Retrieved from www.gov.uk/government/publications/labour-market-projections-for-the-uk (accessed 12 September 2016).

UK Government 2016. "Prove Your Right to Live in the UK as an EU Citizen". Retrieved from www.gov.uk/help/about-govuk (accessed 24 October 2016).

United Nations 2015. "Trends in International Migrant Stock: Migrants by Destination and Origin". Retrieved from www.un.org/en/development/desa/population/migration/data/estimates2/estimates15.shtml (accessed 20 September 2016).

Wadsworth, J., S. Dhingra, G. Ottaviano & J. Van Reenen 2016. *Brexit and the Impact of Immigration on the UK*. London: Centre for Economic Performance. Retrieved from http://cep.lse.ac.uk/pubs/download/brexit05.pdf (accessed 12 September 2016).

Waring, P., A. De Ruyter & J. Burgess 2006. "The Australian Fair Pay Commission: Rationale, Operation, Antecedents and Implications". *Economic and Labour Relations Review* **16**(2): 127–46.

Zeffman, H. 2016. "Juncker: No Special Deal After Brexit". *The Times* (26 July). Retrieved from www.thetimes.co.uk/article/juncker-no-special-deal-after-brexit-0b6xvg32x (accessed 24 October 2016).

PART II

TERRITORIAL DIMENSIONS OF BREXIT

CHAPTER 6

THE *EXIT* CONNECTION: EUROPE'S NEW POLANYIAN MOMENT

Dimitris P. Sotiropoulos and John Milios

> Aye, make yourself a plan
> They need you at the top!
> Then make yourself a second plan
> Then let the whole thing drop.
> > Bertolt Brecht, "Song of the Insufficiency of
> > Human Endeavour", *The Threepenny Opera*

INTRODUCTION: CONVERGENCE AND VARIATIONS

In this chapter, we attempt to draw some lessons from Greece that might be applicable to the Brexit debate and the political economy of the post-Brexit era.[1] The use of the term "exit" to describe a possible walk-out from the Eurozone (or the European Union) was initially coined in the case of Greece. For many years, in the wake of the Greek sovereign debt crisis, Grexit has been usually linked to the (additionally) negative economic and political consequences that an exit from the Eurozone would imply. Some economists, commentators and political analysts saw Grexit as inevitable; a few tried to see the exit as a positive scenario or a radical/simple solution to the Greek predicament. For the majority of the relevant discussions and analyses, the Grexit scenario was mostly seen as the "nuclear option", to use Krugman's pessimistic expression (Krugman 2012).

The announcement of a forthcoming UK referendum by David Cameron after the elections in May 2015 automatically boosted a new "exit" term: this time it was Brexit. But in many different respects the UK is not like Greece,

---

1. This chapter was mostly written before the 2016 US Presidential Election. In many respects, the result verifies the main points of our analysis.

so Brexit took different meanings and developed its own political dynamics as a term in public discussions and debates. The UK is a key G7 economy. It is not part of the Eurozone. It has its own currency and an independent central bank. Its international economic and political role is unquestionably very different from that of Greece. The UK did not suffer a severe sovereign debt crisis; on the contrary, after the 2008 global financial meltdown, government borrowing costs reached historically low levels that, in practical terms, increased the fiscal space of the Treasury.[2] The UK's EU membership referendum took place at a period of relative economic prosperity and, despite the outcome, the future growth prospects in the short to medium term are still positive. The UK, like Greece, has for some time experienced twin deficits; that is, both a current account deficit and a government budget deficit. In the case of Greece most analyses argued that a twin deficit country could not survive within the Eurozone unless structural reforms were immediately imposed (without, of course, explaining that the reasons for the problem related to the architecture of the euro). The arguments from the Greek case cannot easily be used in the case of the UK, and a hypothetical disentanglement from the EU looked much less impractical, at least at first sight. Yet the former UK Chancellor of the Exchequer, George Osborne, used the experience of the Greek economy to create scare stories in order to justify further austerity in the UK.

From the beginning of the Greek crisis the authors of this chapter have argued against an exit from the Eurozone (Milios & Sotiropoulos 2011; Sotiropoulos *et al.* 2013). This standpoint is by no means a defence of the current form of the common currency or status quo. The line of the argument is that Grexit could not, in any possible way, improve the living conditions of the working class in Greece. In the very short term, given all sorts of transitional impracticalities and hazards, it would definitely provoke a further economic shock. All domestic accounts would have to be transferred into a new national currency, which would have led to a free fall in its value. The new exchange rate would then create a huge balance sheet mismatch and force Greece to default on all of its external public and private debt, causing further recession and leaving the economy temporarily without any meaningful financial intermediation. In the medium term, Grexit would also imply a labour devaluation project. It would constitute a more violent market-based alternative to the existing political agenda of a large real depreciation in the

---

2. The annual long-term interest rates, which indicate the borrowing costs of the government and the overall country specific risk, fell from 5.1 per cent in 2007 to 1.8 per cent in 2015 (data from Ameco, https://data.europa.eu/euodp/en/data/dataset/ameco, accessed 29 December 2016).

form of continued negative wage growth. In the face of strong inflationary pressures, real wages would have to keep up with a falling exchange rate for the current account to readjust. Greece would also need international reserves to service its current account deficit, which would additionally deepen due to the post-Grexit disruption of the capital inflows and currency devaluation. This would imply a new memorandum, probably with the International Monetary Fund, if not the EU; the terms would be devastating and Greece's negotiating position would be very weak (if the Eurozone survived Grexit). Sovereign debt negotiations would bring Greece to the very same negotiating table with existing European creditors without any leverage this time. The new economic shock would boost extreme right-wing ideas and structures of power, so Greek society would probably suffer great losses both in economic and political terms (i.e. workers' benefits, protections and civil rights). All in all, our argument was not pro-euro but an anti-Grexit one.

The UK is very different from Greece and the above argument is not directly applicable here, but there may be some similarities. The Brexit agenda is not going to improve the condition of the working people. It practically implies the attempt to establish a labour devaluation strategy on the basis of right-wing xenophobic conservative social consensus to the benefit of the political and economic elites. Parts of UK capital might find a "hard" Brexit as unnecessarily risky or ambiguous. No one can be sure, at this point, of the final outcome of the ongoing negotiations. However, the state as the underwriter of capital always expresses and guarantees the political unity of the capitalist class regardless of inter-capital disputes and contradictions (Milios & Sotiropoulos 2009). And the current social correlation of power in the UK points towards a risky right-wing leap towards the global market that despite its "adjustment" costs would articulate the new long-term platform for UK capitalism.

ANTI-IMMIGRATION SENTIMENT AS THE DECISIVE FACTOR OF THE REFERENDUM RESULT

Generations of Tory politicians and party members have been politically raised to see Britain's EU membership as a doomed marriage. This expression is actually borrowed from the title of Daniel Hannan's brief pamphlet, which attempted to explain the Brexit case to the public (Hannan 2016). Hannan defended the Brexit agenda against any accusation of nationalism or populism. For him, Brexit is a critical and manageable first step towards economic prosperity and more democracy by parting with a bureaucratic European Union; the latter is mostly represented as a set of irrational and restrictive regulations undemocratically imposed by Brussels (ibid.). In a similar fashion, Nigel Lawson, the former Chancellor of the Exchequer and another well-known Tory Eurosceptic, argued that Brexit would let the UK become, under a proper Tory leadership, "the most dynamic and freest country in the whole of Europe" (Lawson 2016). As a matter of fact, there has always been strong Euroscepticism within UK economic and political elites. Hannan's and Lawson's arguments echo Bernard Connolly's 1995 book with the telling title *The Rotten Heart of Europe: The Dirty War for Europe's Money*. This book argued that the European exchange rate mechanism, the predecessor of the Euro, was an indispensable part of a political project to undermine the political and economic sovereignty of European countries (Connolly 1995). This trend has been reinforced by the establishment and rise of the UK Independence Party (UKIP), which has politically outflanked the conventional stance of the Conservative Party.

There is no question that a right-wing shift and return to conservative Thatcherism have been the driving inspiration among Tory Brexiteers and a significant part of their supporters. After all, about 60 per cent of Tory voters defied David Cameron's leadership and the gloomy post-Brexit economic perspective offered by his Chancellor, George Osborne (see Lord Ashcroft 2016). For the Brexiteers, Europe is not pro-capital enough and UK political influence is insufficient to put the whole EU on a modern Thatcherite track. However, the decisive factor of the outcome of the referendum was not the pro-capital agenda but the gradually rising anti-immigration and xenophobic sentiment, a card that, admittedly, was played really well by the Brexit camp. Immigration control, as a critical part of the "reclaim" of sovereignty, was one of the key reasons that many traditional Tory and Labour voters, for whom UKIP has become an attractive alternative, chose to support the Leave campaign (*ibid.*).

In the General Election of 2015, Cameron attacked the Opposition Labour Party by warning that a Labour government would mean a "return to uncontrolled immigration", which would threaten social cohesion and put pressure on public services and wages. This enabled the pro-austerity and anti-EU immigration discourse to dominate the electoral debates with little rebuttal from other political parties, with the exception of the Scottish Nationalist Party (SNP) in Scotland. Tory political dominance in the UK was based on an ideological narrative that *succeeded in associating xenophobia with the Conservative anti-Labour agenda*. In this narrative, any anti-austerity political demand was not just ineffective and futile, it was primarily presented as opposing the British national interest.

In the UK, the Remain campaign failed to address a strong and convincing anti-austerity argument. Neither the Remain nor the Leave campaign presented Britain as an essential part of the EU project. People were requested to decide whether EU membership was a good *instrument* for the national interest. Dissatisfaction with the government *within* the dominant political discourse soon boosted the hopes of Brexiteers. The rise of xenophobia was the decisive factor for the Leave vote. Cameron's plan was defeated, but the message the people sent to Westminster was not an anti-austerity one, (that still has some popular support among the poorest areas). Anti-immigration rhetoric gave the Tories their chance to attempt a new Thatcherite revolution, and also to reclaim political territory back from UKIP. This explains the exemplary smooth transition to a new Cabinet led by Theresa May. Quite ironically the defeat of Cameron empowered the Tory political strategy to give rise to a new plan. Cameron became the sacrificed *Iphigenia*[3] to the benefit of the Thatcherite agenda, a victim of his own ideological victory. This is also in line with the Greek experience in the wake of the sovereign debt crisis: the conservative ideological hegemony of the right generously offered the ground for the rise of fascism and its political formations when things stopped becoming smooth for the political establishment.

IS THE RISE OF FAR-RIGHT AND ANTI-IMMIGRATION SENTIMENT ALL OVER EUROPE A THREAT TO NEOLIBERALISM?

Is the rise of xenophobia a threat to neoliberalism?[4] Strangely enough, the answer is no. This is one of the big lessons to be drawn from the Greek political and economic crisis. The rise of the neo-Nazi party Golden Dawn has never been an actual threat to the conservative agenda and related neoliberal economic and social reforms. In spite of its superficial anti-establishment rhetoric, Golden Dawn has proved a valuable political ally to austerity policies. Its role has been complementary to post-crisis authoritarian governance, blocking electoral shifts to the left, attacking immigrants and trade unionists, targeting mass social movements, and supporting key pro-capital law making in the parliament. In other words, Golden Dawn has provided

---

3. In Greek mythology Iphigenia, the daughter of King Agamemnon, was sacrificed by her father so his ships could sail to Troy.

4. Neoliberalism belongs to this category of terms, in which their wide use deprive them of a clear analytical content. For us, neoliberalism is briefly a synonym to globalization as the irreversible new form of capitalism: it involved a fundamental re-contextualization of the relationships between capitalist states, the workings of capital and the exposure to global markets driven by the financial flow of capital world-wide. Of course, many implications emerge from this general definition. For more details on our argument, see Sotiropoulos *et al.* (2013).

useful support to the political status quo. In fact, this is the strategic role of the contemporary far-right political forces all over the western world. As long as the conservative neoliberal agenda works and produces results, an ideological empowerment of the "nation" against any hypothetical "foreign" threat is a useful political formula to subordinate working-class interests to a pro-capital strategy. In other words, the current rise of anti-immigration sentiment neither poses a threat to the free movement of capital nor, in practical terms, could decisively tighter control of immigration flows. To use Marxist terminology, xenophobia sets forth a form of capitalist governance model that subsumes and subordinates a resistant and gradually dissatisfied working people to a conservative pro-capital strategy (Sotiropoulos *et al.* 2013). How this will pan out in the rest of the EU is an open question.

The rise of far-right political forces is a sign of deeper political shifts in contemporary capitalist societies. This rise indicates that extreme right-wing ideas have become more appealing and that the whole political spectrum is moving to the right. Working people do worry about the disintegration of the welfare state, the rise of income and social inequalities, the crisis of the health and pension system, etc., but they gradually redirect blame on "foreigners" and foreign political "centres of power", looking to the empowerment of domestic power structures as the only possible solution. In this sense, they end up supporting the political agenda that was responsible for the deterioration of their living conditions in the first place. In this vicious circle, Europe and the Western world might look as though it is drifting back to the turbulent 1930s. However, this time things seem a little bit different. Some time ago, Karl Polanyi argued that authoritarian governments in the 1930s were the answer to working-class political unrest in a market society that refused to function (Polanyi 1992). Unlike then, globalization today is irreversible. However, the Western world might still be heading towards its new Polanyian moment. Quasi-nationalisms look like an effective way to tame and control working class unrest without the need to abandon the strategic free market ideal.

The above line of reasoning answers to the apparent contradiction with regard to the Brexit referendum: people attempting to send a strong message of disobedience to the Westminster establishment wound up supporting the most conservative UK government after the Thatcherism of the 1980s. This interpretation goes beyond the explanations attempting to understand the voting behaviour in the Brexit case on the basis of purely economic criteria – the winners and losers from globalization. In fact, "for every one person who voted leave because the global rat race had left them behind, there was more than one person pretty well served by the economy, who voted leave" (Williams 2016). If we look at the figures that plot voting against housing, social and council tenants voted Leave, but so did those who owned their houses outright, the people we might describe as society's winners. By housing type, the only groups where Remain prevailed were private renters and people with mortgages (*ibid.*).

The above analysis can be easily generalized across Europe. Following the election of Donald Trump as the President of the United States, forthcoming election results (in France, and Germany) might see the rise of right-wing parties adding some more confusion to the already dysfunctional monetary union but they will not pose a real threat to capital and its free movement. Most importantly, it seems that the xenophobic Brexit agenda is gradually haunting all of Europe. All European leaders have warned that the UK will not be allowed to "cherry-pick" the relationship to the single market (SEM). The price to be paid is EU immigration. Suddenly, immigration flows and free labour movement has become the negative cost one needs to pay in order to "enjoy" access to the single market. The rising anti-immigration sentiment has also added heavily to the stalemate with regard to the Syrian refugee crisis. Europe has gradually become unwilling to develop common responses to big humanitarian challenges of our time, further exposing its fundamental weaknesses.

THE STRATEGIC DILEMMA OF THE LEFT: SOME THOUGHTS FOR THE FUTURE

In the UK referendum the left and the Labour Party, in particular, were caught in the midst of a dangerous and unpleasant dilemma. Both the Remain and the Leave campaigns were led by opposing political forces. UKIP and conservative Tories put their stamp on the Leave camp, while other Tories, Liberal Democrats and Labour Party Blairites led the Remain campaign. The ground for the Labour Party under Corbyn's leadership was particularly slippery in that debate. The challenge for the left was more strategic: would it be possible to argue for a left-wing exit (the so-called Lexit) when Brexit is ideologically ruled by Thatcher's admirers or nationalists? Would it be possible to uncritically support the current version of the EU, which is nothing more than a stronghold of neoliberal recession-led reforms? The argument that was finally adopted, "remain to change Europe", was hardly appealing and convincing. There was no attempt to challenge the xenophobic charge that unless the UK exited the EU, it would become like Greece, as was the case in respect of austerity.

The UK political establishment has so far been an absolute and uncompromising guarantor of a right-wing and pro-market EU. It has also been an impediment to further unification, which could potentially rebalance the current dominance of the conservative political agenda. The UK could change Europe in so far as it changed itself. The "remain and change" line would make sense only to the extent that it set out an alternative agenda for both UK and EU politics. This project was never actually undertaken by the left. And there is a good reason for that.

The Labour Party right-wingers have put forward a clear argument about Britain's EU membership: staying close to Europe would serve the national interest, empowering the role of the UK in the contemporary global landscape. On the other hand, the left-wing perspective about the EU can be summarized by the following statement made by Labour MP Tony Benn during the UK's 1975 European Communities membership referendum:

> When I saw how the European Union was developing, it was very obvious what they had in mind was not democratic. In Britain, you vote for a government so the government has to listen to you, and if you don't like it you can change it. (BBC 2014)

Tony Benn was correct in indicating the democratic deficit in the way the EU has been developed so far. However, a possible answer to this deficit could, in principle, be a demand for more unification: the European parliament to become legitimate and accountable in its decision-making. Tony Benn was against that prospect because he seemed to believe that it was easier for voters to influence national governments. The current Labour Party leadership sympathizes with this view, and this probably explains its unwillingness to whole-heartedly support the Remain campaign. It is also the same argument that inspired the Lexit idea that a left-wing Brexit was possible. However, this argument is based on two erroneous assumptions with regard to the social nature of the capitalist state. First, the capitalist state and its political institutions are not neutral; the state is a key institution in the organization of capitalist power. Second, capitalist states and societies cannot exist in isolation. Their complex and multi-level and multi-scalar interactions are reflected in domestic power relations and structures. The UK's "hard" exit from the EU would not solve the above mentioned democratic gap in relation to EU membership to the extent that the UK would enter into other trade agreements winding up with similar or worse "sovereignty compromises" in the global market. Hard Brexit would imply a recalibration of the UK's position at the international level, consolidating a more conservative political agenda and related conservative forms of governance. It would probably imply more sovereignty concessions always to the benefit of British political and economic elites. A different set of compromises would originate a new democratic deficit. As was mentioned in the introduction to this chapter, the same argument applies to the case of Greece. The UK's Official Opposition could learn from the case of Greece that in globalized capitalism there is no way to reclaim "full sovereignty" even for countries like the UK. An exit from political unions could easily result in higher "sovereignty losses" always to the strategic benefit of domestic elites: this type of sovereign "concessions" practically indicates the inability of working classes to influences decision making.

The question with regard to the exit from the EU should thus be addressed in relation to an analysis of the contemporary form of capitalism. The exit from the EU could not be a return to the nation-state in general but only a decisive step towards a different interplay of power relations and an alternative interaction with the global market. Should Brexit be a strategic target for the working classes and the left? Could an alternative progressive exposure to the global market exist, to the interest of working people? Some progressive thinkers do embrace this idea, which gains some ground even within Germany, probably the most pro-European society. For instance, acknowledging that the Eurozone has been a political mistake, Wolfgang Streeck suggests unravelling the euro project and returning to an orderly system of flexible exchange rates in Europe (Streeck 2014).[5] It is clear that in the absence of fiscal federalism within the Eurozone then peripheral economies have borne the brunt of the pursuit of austerity. This is certainly the experience of Greece but the fundamental issue is whether the EU can hold together. Ironically, the Greek model may be one that the UK regrets emulating if the long-term consequences of Brexit are as damaging as many are currently beginning to realize.

Globalization is something much more than a mutual institutional contract between sovereign nation-states that can be unilaterally challenged. Globalization is the *irreversible* new form of capitalism. The reproduction of social power relations is intertwined with the workings and the historical norms of globalization (Sotiropoulos *et al.* 2013). Even if the project of European Monetary Union (EMU) were abandoned, individual European societies would not have the historical option or even the power to place them beyond the reach of globalization. The argument holds for countries like Greece, but also for others like the UK.

No doubt the EMU has been for many countries a useful mechanism to facilitate the adjustment to a new global order by promoting and reinforcing conservative reforms. The case of Greece is probably the most indicative example. However, the exit from the EU could by no means become part of a genuine deglobalizing process. It would probably impose upon societies a

---

5. See also the appeal of the Lexit campaign at http://lexit-network.org/appeal. Of course, the debate in Germany has many different aspects as well (see Offe 2015; Habermas 2015).

more conservative pro-capital agenda, one led by a new exposure to global competition. As a matter of fact, the aggressive and conservative ruling elites of the UK got it right. An exit from the EU implies exposure to a competitive global market, in which what was claimed and promised by Brexiteers as "more flexibility" means, in practical terms, nothing other than a set of the doomed Transatlantic Trade and Investment Partnership (TTIP)-like bilateral type of agreements (exactly like the one recently agreed between Canada and the EU). It might be a risky strategy but, as argued above, it is one that can potentially subordinate social resistance to a new conservative strategy for UK capitalism. *Mutatis mutandis*, this also holds in the case of Greece.

The Leave or Remain dilemma is a systemic one: it is primarily about which pro-capital strategy British politics will follow from now on. This is a wrong debate for the left. The improvement of the living conditions of the working class could only come from a challenge of domestic power structures and the creation of radical democratic institutions in an anti-capitalist perspective. The Brexit agenda in that sense might take a range of different forms, but is definitely here to stay. It cannot be reversed but it can be defeated.

REFERENCES

BBC 2014. "Tony Benn: His Views on Socialism, Europe, War and Writing". *BBC News* (14 March). Retrieved from www.bbc.co.uk/news/uk-politics-26575258 (accessed 29 December 2016).

Brecht, B. 1979. *The Threepenny Opera* (trans. R. Manheim & J. Willett). London: Bloomsbury.

Connolly, B. 1995. *The Rotten Heart of Europe: The Dirty War for Europe's Money.* London: Faber & Faber.

Habermas, J. 2015. *The Lure of Technocracy.* Cambridge: Polity.

Hannan, D. 2016. *A Doomed Marriage: Why Britain Should Leave the EU.* London: Notting Hill.

Krugman, P. 2012. "European Crisis Realities". *New York Times* (25 February). Retrieved from http://krugman.blogs.nytimes.com/2012/02/25/european-crisis-realities (accessed 29 December 2016).

Lawson, N. 2016. "Thanks to Brexit We Can Finish the Thatcher Revolution". *Financial Times* (3 September): 12.

Lord Ashcroft (2016) "How the United Kingdom Voted on Thursday... and Why". *Lord Ashcroft Polls* (24 June). Retrieved from http://lordashcroftpolls.com/2016/06/how-the-united-kingdom-voted-and-why (accessed 29 December 2016).

Milios, J. & D. P. Sotiropoulos 2009. *Rethinking Imperialism.* Abingdon: Routledge.

Milios, J. & D. P. Sotiropoulos 2011. *Imperialism, Financial Markets and Crisis.* Athens: Nisos Publications [in Greek].

Offe, C. 2015. *Europe Entrapped*. Cambridge: Polity.

Polanyi, K. 1992. *The Great Transformation: The Political and Economic Origins of Our Time*. Boston, MA: Beacon Press.

Sotiropoulos, D. P., J. Milios & S. Lapatsioras 2013. *A Political Economy of Contemporary Capitalism and its Crisis: Demystifying Finance*. Abingdon: Routledge.

Streeck, W. 2014. *Buying Time: The Delayed Crisis of Democratic Capitalism*. London: Verso.

Williams, Z. 2016. "Think the North and the Poor Caused Brexit? Think Again". *The Guardian* (7 August). Retrieved from www.theguardian.com/commentisfree/2016/aug/07/north-poor-brexit-myths (accessed 29 December 2016).

CHAPTER 7

A SCOTTISH PERSPECTIVE: CHARTING A PATH THROUGH THE RUBBLE

Jim Gallagher

A few months after the EU membership referendum, governments in London, Edinburgh and elsewhere are still struggling to find a way through the mess that an ill-considered referendum and a notably mendacious campaign have created. In so doing they should most obviously pursue the national interest, but partisan interests remain on the agenda in both London and Edinburgh. This chapter offers advice to both the UK and Scottish governments, and focuses particularly on the challenge the vote has produced to the territorial integrity of the United Kingdom.

WHAT THE VOTE MEANS, AND WHAT IT DOESN'T MEAN

The Leave vote was as much protest as proposition, like the campaign which promoted it. It cannot be ignored, but it must also be understood. Support for leaving the EU was strong among those, especially older voters, long suspicious of European entanglements and influence, but also among economically disadvantaged communities and poorer people. Together they (just) added up to a majority. There is a striking resemblance to the Scottish independence referendum. Not just that both were nationalist in tone, though Brexiteers were for "taking back control",[1] while "decisions about Scotland taken by the people who care most about Scotland"[2] was the SNP's best argument, but in the composition of the vote. In Scotland, long-standing nationalist support, ideologically committed to leaving the UK, was supplemented

---

1. See, for example, www.voteleavetakecontrol.org.
2. "The most important decisions about our economy and society will be taken by the people who care most about Scotland, that is by the people of Scotland" (Scottish Government 2013: 7).

by the votes of those who thought the present economic and constitutional setup did not serve their interests and had left them behind (e.g. see Curtice 2014); they thought change could make things no worse for them, and were told it would make them better. Similarly, in the European referendum those with a long-standing ideological opposition to or discomfort with Europe were bolstered by a group of voters whose alienation from the political process and dissatisfaction with their economic situation made them receptive to a message that with one bound they would be free. Voters who think things can't get worse are not persuaded by warnings of risk. The relative proportions of voters in each case is the subject of reasonable argument, but in both a substantial share of the vote for change was a negative, dissatisfaction with the status quo – and that's what delivered the narrow Brexit majority, not endorsement of a particular plan for the UK's international status.

Not least because, as we all now know, there was no plan. The Leave camp had no specific proposition to put before the electorate: it was a simple in/out vote with no choice as to how "out" might be achieved. Voters did not know whether they were opting to become Norway, Canada or Australia with respect to the EU. Indeed (in echoes of the Scottish campaign) they were promised things likely to be mutually inconsistent: like retaining free trade but abandoning free movement of people. So voters were told that the UK would remain in a single market stretching from Iceland to Albania,[3] while also controlling migration. David Davis announced afterwards this was unlikely to be true.[4] After six months of apparent indecision Theresa May announced that the UK would in fact leave the single market.

Governments must nevertheless be guided by the result. If you hold a referendum, you must expect many voters to answer the question at the front of their minds, not the one on the ballot paper. (Voters are like students who answer the question they would like to have been asked, rather than the one on the exam paper. It's the question-setters who failed this exam.) But understanding the vote nevertheless has implications for how governments should proceed. First, it means Prime Minister Theresa May was required to adopt neither the premises or the promises of the Leave campaign. She was under no obligation to adopt the beliefs of the Leave campaign – about, say, the economic effects of change, or how other European governments will react to the vote. Nor was she under any obligation to deliver all the differing promises of the various Leave actors about how leaving the EU should be

---

3. According to Michael Gove (e.g. see Wright 2016).
4. "The simple truth is that if a requirement of membership is giving up control of our borders, then I think that makes that very improbable" (Mr David Davis, Hansard, 5 September 2016, col. 54).

pursued, what the future UK–EU relationship should be, notably in relation to freedom of movement, nor the effects on public spending. The Leave vote was not the endorsement of a manifesto.

The UK government is mandated to pursue Brexit, but does not have to wear Mr Farage's spectacles or keep Mr Gove's promises. Rather it has lost none of its obligations to view the world rationally and pursue the national interest. The same applies to the Scottish government, as discussed further below. Events since the vote suggest that both are driven at least as much by partisan interest.

WHAT THE UK GOVERNMENT SHOULD DO

By announcing his resignation as prime minister, David Cameron at least prevented immediate triggering of the formal legal process for the United Kingdom to leave the EU, the so-called Article 50 notification. Just as well. The process of Article 50, with a two year drop dead date, is designed to make it difficult for departing countries to secure their interest as against those of continuing member states. Mrs May should not be bounced either. Instead, before triggering Article 50 – though it may infuriate some other EU states – the UK should formulate its position, and then ascertain whether that position is achievable in negotiation or, if not, what is. Mrs May has now indicated this will happen by end of March 2017 (BBC 2016): whether the outline position recently announced by Mrs May is in the national interest or achievable in negotiation is presently the subject of intense debate.

In formulating that position, the government must have regard to two key aspects of the UK national interest. First and manifestly, the economic effect, notably on trade with what is Britain's largest market. The second, which has received insufficient attention at UK level as yet, is the implications of the *terms* of exit, as well as the fact of exit, for the territorial integrity of the United Kingdom. The two are closely connected, and must be considered together. By getting both wrong, the government could turn the UK into a group of impoverished, isolated statelets on the fringe of western Europe.

THE ARGUMENT FOR THE EUROPEAN ECONOMIC AREA

We begin with trade. Economists since David Ricardo and Adam Smith have been clear about the economic benefits of free trade. Leaving aside, perhaps, the position of developing countries entering a globalized market (Chang

97

2010), it is clear that free trade brings economic benefits to all who participate in it. That is why governments worldwide continually seek to negotiate free trade agreements, though concerns about the effects on individual sectors, domestic pressure groups and so on, make such negotiations extremely slow and problematic. After many decades, the European Union has achieved not just a customs union but a functioning single market, with free trade in goods, and at least some free trade in relation to services. Free trade is more than just the absence of tariffs, though they matter; the absence of non-tariff barriers which can also be critical – ask any seller of financial services. Ironically enough this was very much a British project, championed initially by Mrs Thatcher.

The economic benefits the single market brings to the UK, and the risks from losing it, were clearly set out in thorough economic analysis by HM Treasury during the referendum campaign (HM Treasury 2016). The over-whelming majority of economists agreed with them. Even if the way in which the work was used in the campaign was unwise, the underlying analysis remains valid. No responsible UK government – however mandated by a referendum vote – can disregard it.

One practicable way of retaining the present level of free trade with the countries of the European Union is by joining not just the customs union but the European Economic Area (EEA), like Norway or Iceland. It is a fantasy to imagine that the UK could negotiate its own, bespoke, free trade agreement with the EU in any reasonable timeframe; it would be the grossest of irresponsibility to assert that in any but the very longest of terms – during which, as Keynes reminded us, we are all dead – abandoning free trade in the EU single market would be economically beneficial to the UK. Achieving Norwegian status or something close to it, therefore, should be the sensible negotiating objective of the UK government. So their first responsibility is to assess whether this can be achieved in negotiation. It may not be achievable but, if it is, it is highly likely that it would be only on the terms in which Norway already enjoys: free movement of labour, alongside the movement of goods, services and capital. That is the nature of the EU single market and the EEA today. Leave campaigners claimed that single market access could be secured without accepting freedom of movement but that does not make it true.

Mrs May and her Brexit Ministers have said that she will not accept that in negotiation. Leave enthusiasts describe it as staying in the EU by the back door, which Mrs May has ruled out (Asthana 2016). But that does not oblige the government to reject free trade when it becomes clear that freedom of movement is an ineluctable concomitant. Nevertheless, that is the approach which the UK government seems determined to follow.

THE TERRITORIAL INTEGRITY OF THE UK

The above is closely connected to the territorial implications of change. It matters most of all for Northern Ireland, and the government must consider this point most carefully. If EEA-style freedom of movement of labour remains, it is easier to retain the common travel area between Britain and Ireland, and so avoid having a hard border for people between the Republic of Ireland and Northern Ireland, or a hard border between Northern Ireland and the rest of the UK. UK ministers' apparent determination to leave the European customs union creates problems for the border to which no solution is obvious. Failure to secure both free trade and freedom of movement has significant economic risks for Northern Ireland and the Republic. It also puts the border back into Irish politics in the way in which it has not been present since 1972, with unpredictable consequences.

Whether the UK remains in the EEA also has implications for the position of Scotland. In one sense, it makes the possibility of an independent Scotland inside the EU with the rest of the UK outside more plausible. If Scotland were independent, there would be an international border on the island of Britain. But if the UK were a member of the EEA, it would not be necessary to construct a new Hadrian's Wall, the original hard border between England and Scotland. People would have the right to move freely. And if the UK remained in the customs union, there would be no need for customs posts at Carlisle. It is far from certain that an independent Scotland in the EU is an achievable aim (whether desirable or not) and the EEA option secures for Scotland many of the advantages of EU membership. It might also open up further, more imaginative, options which are discussed below.

There might be those in England who would claim that arguing for EEA membership to secure the position of Northern Ireland, and to offer a degree of optionality to Scotland, is the tail wagging the dog. But the economic arguments point in exactly the same direction. Others will point out that this result, which meets the referendum mandate, greatly reduces Britain's power in Europe while retaining many of its obligations, but a responsible government will be making the best of a bad job. Whether the government then ask the people again if they are quite sure about leaving now they know what it really means is a different question, beyond the scope of this chapter.

WHAT THE SCOTTISH GOVERNMENT SHOULD DO

The formal position of Scotland is quite clear. It is part of the United Kingdom, a decision confirmed by the Scottish people only two years ago. The UK is the

99

EU member state, and if it ceases to belong to the EU, so does Scotland. That is the central expectation, but the politics are more complex. The SNP administration has wavered on the issue, initially saying that another independence referendum was highly likely, then that it depends on the terms of exit, notably whether Scotland remains in the single market. At her party conference in October 2016, Nicola Sturgeon said "I am determined that Scotland will have the ability to reconsider the question of independence – and to do so before the UK leaves the EU – if that is necessary to protect our country's interests" (Sturgeon 2016). Since then Sturgeon has edged ever closer to demanding another independence referendum, but Holyrood has no legal power to hold such a referendum without UK sanction. It could however seek a political denouement by trying to hold one.

It may be that all that is holding the SNP back is that there is no certainty of winning. Opinion polling suggested Scottish sentiment shifted a little after the vote, but hardly decisively, and obviously not on a sustained basis. It has now (in autumn 2016) returned to the levels seen in the 2014 referendum;[5] and the polls suggest that Scottish voters do not want a rerun (Smith 2016). Indeed independence is some respects a harder sell in 2016 than 2014: Scotland's fiscal position is notably weaker, and its EU status even less certain now than then. The SNP's plan for sharing a currency with the rest of the UK after independence was heavily criticized during the campaign: it is even less easy to envisage if, *ex hypothesi*, an independent Scotland were in the EU while the UK was out. Major issues also arise about the status of the border between Scotland and England, whose nature depends on the terms of EU membership.

At the time of writing Nicola Sturgeon has argued for the whole UK to remain in the single market, or alternatively for Scotland to do so even if the UK does not. The former approach has been rejected by the UK government, and the latter seems undeliverable, although it it still formally under discussion between governments. Rhetoric about a repeated referendum has reached new levels.

A responsible Scottish government however would be seeking to draw lessons from the EU referendum campaign and analysing as objectively as possible where Scotland's national interest lay, in a radically changed environment.

---

5. In May 2016, for example, opinion was 54% to 46% in favour of remaining in the UK (excluding 5% "don't knows"; data from www.whatscotlandthinks.org).

MORE THE SAME THAN DIFFERENT

One immediate reaction – that the vote shows Scotland and England are radically different places – can immediately be put to rest. If a significant proportion of the anti-European majority is an expression of dissatisfaction with the economic and political state of the country, then there is little difference between Scotland and England. Nearly half of Scots voted to reject the UK, and just over half the English population felt the same way about the EU. It would be a mistake to draw too much from the wording of the exam paper, when many voters answered a different question. And it should not be forgotten that a million Scots voted to agree with the majority in England, many of them in the poorest and most disadvantaged communities – and many of them SNP voters. So the conclusion that England and Scotland are different ignores the evidence that they are in many respects just the same. In both countries, many people are hurting, and looking for someone to blame for it. South of the border, Brussels gets the blame; north of it, London.

SCOTLAND'S INTERESTS

Today Scotland belongs to two unions, and, in the view of this author, gets advantages from both. Any Scottish government must try to retain as many of the advantages of both as possible. That is where the interests of Scotland lie, whatever the ideological position of the SNP administration might be. It is to Nicola Sturgeon's credit that she did not simply default to her ideological stance. The challenge for the Scottish government is identifying, in the uncertain position of the UK, how best to safeguard the Scottish interest. They have to consider some very concrete questions: freedom of movement for Scots across borders, most notably with England, but also with the EU; Scotland's trade, today overwhelmingly with England, but significant with the EU; Scotland's fiscal position, currently supported by very large transfers from the rest of the UK and very little from the EU; Scotland's currency; Scotland's defence; and softer issues such as its cultural and social ties. Given the vote, it's not easy to see how all of these can be sustained as they are today, but the obligation is to try.

Trade and freedom of movement go together, and UK membership of the EEA would be overwhelmingly in Scotland's interest, whether independent or still in the UK. It guarantees continued trade with *both* the UK *and* the European Union. Moreover, it is the only way to be sure that people in Scotland will be able to continue to live and work *both* in the British Isles *and* mainland Europe as they can today; and it safeguards the position of

EU citizens here and UK citizens elsewhere in the EU. The Scottish government's single most important priority therefore should be to press the UK as hard as possible to take the Norway option or something very close to it. If it cannot be achieved, Scotland faces the choice of a hard border at a European airport (if in the UK) or a hard border at a new Hadrian's Wall (if in the EU). A new Hadrian's Wall along the Cheviots is just about the worst outcome for Scottish trade, and for the 400,000 Scots who live in England, and the 200,000 English people living in Scotland.

Scotland's fiscal position was extensively explored during the referendum campaign, and has changed significantly for the worse since then, as North Sea oil revenues are now essentially zero, and unlikely to be significant in the foreseeable future. There are some unpalatable facts here, which cannot be ignored. Scotland's fiscal deficit is huge, proportionately twice the UK's already very large deficit, and even if the UK were to manage to get into surplus – now very unlikely in the next few years – Scotland would not. Public spending on the services run by the Scottish Parliament is roughly 25 per cent per head higher than in England. This is financed by fiscal transfers of around £7 billion per annum from the rest of the UK and supported by the UK government's borrowing capacity. During the independence referendum, Yes-campaigners tried to obfuscate these realities, but oil revenues were never going to fill the gap, and they certainly won't now. Mr John Swinney – who understands the fiscal reality very well – negotiated hard and successfully to ensure that the fiscal transfers to Scotland did not decline when Holyrood got new tax powers. Breaking the UK union would mean losing all those fiscal transfers and Scotland swallowing reductions in public services, benefits and pensions of at least 10 per cent more than the austerity already imposed by the UK government. So the Scottish government's second priority should be to safeguard Scotland's public services, pension and benefit payments, and that means securing a continuing fiscal union with the UK.

The other critical economic choice for Scotland relates to the currency; Brexit is a game-changer here. Nationalists previously argued an independent Scotland could and should continue to use the pound in a formal currency union with the rest of the UK with both in the EU. But with the rest of the UK out, that argument is much harder to make. While it is possible to envisage an independent Scotland using the pound informally, on what is called a "dollarized" basis, this is inconsistent with EU obligations, and likely to create very serious fiscal difficulties indeed: unable to create or print money, a government in those circumstances has to run a surplus in order to accumulate the currency to allow the economy to function. The outcome is similar if a country seeks to tie its currency to an enabling currency through the use of a currency board (as Gibraltar and the Channel Islands do today, and as Ireland did from 1923 until the Irish currency floated in 1979). If Scotland loses the pound, the choice is a new Scottish currency, probably with a promise to use the euro. Just as it is not certain whether and when an independent Scotland could join the EU, so is it not clear when or on what conditions it could join the euro: as it stands, Scotland fails very badly to meet the required fiscal rules. So the most likely option would appear to be a new Scottish currency, which would have to float on the currency markets. Scotland would be in no position to peg it against the pound or the euro as that requires large reserves of hard currency to intervene in the markets. Exchange rate volatility immediately introduces uncertainty into Scotland's trade with *both* the rest of the UK *and* the rest of the EU. One of the big lessons of the independence referendum was that currency unions do not work without fiscal unions, and that if Scotland wants to keep the pound it must keep the UK fiscal union too. This analysis suggests the Scottish government's next priority should be to continue to use the pound in a currency union with the rest of the UK, which will be possible if (and only if) Scotland also remains in a UK fiscal union.

Scotland gets advantages from the EU as well as the UK, and the Scottish government must aim to keep as many of these as possible. Independence with EU membership would do that, but may not be achievable and comes at a significant loss of the UK advantages. The most important EU advantage is free trade, and it can be retained with both the UK and the EU under the EEA or EEA-like option and membership of the customs union also. In the past Scotland has benefited from European structural funds, though this is very much a declining advantage. It also participates in the common agricultural policy, and probably gets proportionately greater payments from it than does the UK as a whole. By contrast, rightly or wrongly, the common fisheries policy is deeply unpopular among Scottish fishermen (e.g. see Lochhead 2009). Like the rest of the UK, Scotland also participates in other EU programmes, such as university research funding and scholarships. A Scottish government's next priority must be to do what it can to clarify all the options for Scotland's relationship with EU in future. Most obviously, if Scotland were independent, could it look forward with certainty to immediate EU membership? If not, the prospects for an independent Scotland are bleak, as a member of neither union. If so, what conditions would attach? More intriguingly, is there any prospect of a continuing relationship between Scotland and the EU if Scotland remains in a union, perhaps an evolved or amended union, with the rest of the UK.

In exploring the scope for Scotland to continue to enjoy some EU relationship, perhaps even if the UK leaves, the Scottish government should explore whether, for example, Scotland could continue to apply EU law in relation to devolved matters, or even whether Scottish citizens could retain European citizenship. What institutional mechanisms might enable Scotland to retain some voice in the councils of the European Union? Would opting out of the common fisheries policy be to Scotland's advantage, and are there alternatives to the common agricultural policy which would meet Scottish needs better than the European system presently in place?

SCOTLAND'S OPTIONS

The range of possible options for Scotland's constitutional position post-Brexit is uncomfortably wide, because of the uncertainty about the UK position and about Scotland's European status. Independence outside the EU, however, is an option that can readily be ruled out: Scotland would lose the advantages of both unions, disobey the mandate of both its referendums and gain nothing. If it seems likely or possible that EU membership is not guaranteed in the event of Scottish independence, then the Scottish government can only put its independence aspirations on hold. Independence with EEA membership only offers mostly disadvantages over remaining in the UK with that status. How attractive an independent Scotland with guaranteed EU membership looks depends on the UK's position. If the UK becomes a third country with respect to the EU, the common travel area might well have to be abolished, and Scotland would be obliged to create a new border for the movement of people and customs. Scotland would become an offshore island of the EU, with virtually no direct travel links with the rest of the union. If, however, the UK followed the Norwegian option, then independence need not require a hard border with England. The choice is then whether giving up a common UK currency, UK fiscal sharing and the other economic and social links with England, Wales and Northern Ireland are offset by representation in the European Parliament and Commission, and participation in the common agricultural policy and common fisheries policy.

If Scotland remains part of the UK, it obviously retains the common travel area, the pound sterling, fiscal sharing and the UK single, domestic market. If the UK is not part of the European single market, then Scotland would simply lose access to it. It is hard to envisage how Scotland can be in the single market, and the customs union, if the UK is not.[6] Scotland can retain many of the advantages of EU membership if the UK joins the EEA, though it loses representation in the European Parliament, and Scots would no longer be EU citizens; nor would Scotland participate in the common agricultural policy

---

6. Michael Keating (2016) argues persuasively that it could not.

and the common fisheries policy. Whether these last two are advantages or disadvantages is a point which might be debated.

It is certainly worth considering whether there are any mechanisms by which Scotland might retain closer links with the European Union while still remaining part of the UK. This makes much more sense if the UK is part of the EEA or something equivalent. As part of the UK Scotland cannot be a member state, represented in the European Parliament and nominating a European Commissioner. But it might seek to become a region outside the EU which was nevertheless associated with it, perhaps with some application of its law, and participation in some of its programmes. So for example, the Scottish Parliament could continue to be obliged, or oblige itself, to follow EU law; UK citizens resident in Scotland could perhaps even stay EU citizens (after all, Greenlanders remain EU citizens even though Greenland left the EU, because Greenland is still part of the Danish realm); Scotland might retain representation on the European Committee of the Regions; in return for some form of subscription fee, its universities might continue to participate in research sharing (as Israel does; see European Commission 2016), and student scholarships. It might even voluntarily sign up to the common fisheries policy.

One option would be for the United Kingdom to make an imaginative constitutional change: to give the devolved administrations in Scotland, Wales and Northern Ireland the power to enter into international agreements with the EU in relation to devolved matters. This would enable the Scottish government, for example, to negotiate continued participation in, say, EU reciprocal health agreements, or Erasmus studentships. It could also buy into EU research programmes, and reciprocal enforcement of, for example, arrest warrants.

If, contrary to the advice in this chapter, the UK government rejects the single market and freedom of movement, another intriguing possibility opens up. Abolishing freedom of movement for labour, on the face of it, would require much stricter border checks at places of entry to the United Kingdom, so the EU citizens will be treated in more or less the same way as citizens of third countries at airports, etc. But this creates almost insoluble practical problems, most especially at the border between Northern Ireland and the Republic. Both governments in Dublin and Edinburgh have reiterated their commitment to be common travel area between Britain and Ireland. But Ireland will also retain freedom of movement with the rest of the EU. So the Northern Irish border would be a back door for EU citizens seeking to enter the United Kingdom. This, together with the real practical problems arising from a large number of EU citizens who now move between Britain and the European mainland, suggests that the UK will agree visa free travel for EU citizens, even as it rejects freedom of movement for labour (see McLean & Gallagher 2016).

The consequence would be a requirement for what is sometimes called "point" control of migration: all EU citizens would be allowed to visit the UK, but they would not be allowed to settle without specific permission. As a result, employers, or perhaps even public service providers and landlords, would have to check people's eligibility to work or settle in the United Kingdom. This control would be, in the jargon, "in-country" rather than at the border. Because it is in-country it can be applied differently in different parts of the UK, and opens up the possibility of different EU migration policies in different nations of the UK – devolving migration, for example, for EU citizens, in Scotland, Northern Ireland or London. Each of them has special and specific migration and demographic issues to manage.

A CONFEDERAL UNITED KINGDOM?

These are of course speculative possibilities, and imply some degree of weakening of the Scotland–UK relationship. Whether they require a fully, formally, federal UK is perhaps arguable. Such an arrangement might, as has often been pointed out, turn out to be unstable in its own right. But it is inevitable that Brexit – whatever its terms – will require substantial alteration to the territorial constitution of the United Kingdom. Many substantial powers will be repatriated from Brussels to but not all of them will come to the UK government. Many of the responsibilities which are currently, perhaps only notionally, devolved such as environmental protection, fisheries, and agriculture, belong by virtue of the devolution settlements to the governments in Edinburgh, Belfast and Cardiff, not simply Westminster.

There may be a temptation for UK ministers simply to seek to arrogate to themselves the powers that Brussels currently exercises in these areas. But this would not only be politically unwise, but constitutionally improper. There has been much loose talk about whether the devolved legislatures can somehow veto Brexit, because leaving the EU affects their powers. This is unrealistic, and unreasonable. But by contrast legislation in Westminster to constrain their powers on matters which are currently devolved but subject to European law would immediately engage the convention that Westminster does not legislate on devolved matters without the consent of the devolved legislature.

As a result, one unintended consequence of Brexit is that the UK's devolved administrations will become markedly more powerful, and the UK government will have to agree common UK policies on such matters as fisheries or agriculture. Of course the UK government will be the most powerful player in such negotiations, but because they are longer dealing with matters of international relations, it will not have the whip hand it has today. New and more effective mechanisms of intergovernmental cooperation and agreement will be needed, and this represents itself a major shift in the balance of power in the UK's territorial constitution. So far as Scotland is concerned, major new powers are already heading in Holyrood's direction – over taxation, welfare and other matters. Added to these – and potentially supplemented by the powers over EU relations and even migration as proposed above – the shift in the balance of power following Brexit is going to lead to quite a different kind of territorial UK. Looked at through the lens of Edinburgh, the UK is already more than merely federal: the range of powers and flexibilities available to the Scottish parliament is in many respects wider and deeper than those available to states and provinces in federal countries. Changes of this sort might take it further, to a constitutional arrangement perhaps better described as confederal. In the view of this author at least this is probably a better plan for Scotland than rerunning the 2014 referendum (Gallagher 2016).

ONE LESSON FROM THE SHAMBLES

The European referendum and its result have put the UK, and Scotland, in a difficult and uncertain situation. The people have voted in the absence of a detailed prospectus hoping for something that probably cannot be delivered in practice; indeed they may find that the only practicable solution is one which they would have rejected had it been offered to them clearly beforehand. This is a perverse result of a referendum: suggesting that referendums are not, perhaps, the gold standard of democracy after all. The UK should not have made that mistake, and Scotland should not make a similar one. The Scottish government have not rushed into another independence referendum, but if there were one it could only be on the basis of a proposition which was guaranteed to be deliverable, which could be put into effect with certainty. So, for example, no responsible Scottish government could promote independence without being sure of Scotland's position in the EU, without knowing the likely position of the rest of the United Kingdom in relation to free movement and trade and without a practicable economic plan for public spending and the currency. Similarly, if there were to be scope for some more imaginative constitutional resolution which retained Scotland-EU links, the full detail would have to be worked out and guaranteed to be delivered before that choice was placed before the population. One bad and ill-informed decision should not lead to another.

In the spirit of not letting a crisis go to waste, it is worth asking whether this time of uncertainty offers an opportunity for Scotland to unite behind a constitutional solution that puts the divisions of 2014 behind it, goes beyond the false dichotomy of nationalism and unionism and focuses on safeguarding the national interest? The Brexit vote was unexpected and unplanned for. Neither the Cameron government nor the Leave campaigners had a plan to be implemented after the British people's decision. The result was not just a change of prime minister and cabinet but six months of near-paralysis in which the government's policy consisted of the tautology that Brexit meant Brexit. Not long before this book went to press, however, three significant developments conditioned what it might mean and its implications for the territorial constitution of the UK. In December 2016, the Scottish government set out its arguments in a paper about Brexit and Scottish independence (Scottish Government 2016); then in January 2017, the Supreme Court produced its judgment on what the UK's constitutional requirements for triggering Article 50 to leave the EU were; the UK government produced a White Paper on its approach (repeating and barely expanding on a prime ministerial speech). These interact.

After initially saying that Brexit of itself justified another Scottish independence referendum, the Scottish government paper took a step back. No referendum would be needed if the UK remained in the single market (as this chapter has argued for); nor would one be needed if Scotland could remain in it even if the UK did not. The Supreme Court's judgment clarified the role of Parliament, but was also made clear that there was no legal obligation to consult Edinburgh before triggering Article 50. The UK government Brexit line was uncompromising: leave the single market, prioritising immigration control over free trade, and probably leave the customs union too. This sets the cat among the devolved pigeons. The Scottish government has ramped up its rhetoric on a referendum as a result (and few find its fall-back plan plausible; Gallagher 2017). Leaving the customs union raises apparently insuperable problems over the border between the North and South of Ireland, and indeed between England and an independent Scotland. A standoff between London and Edinburgh now seems likely. Whether this will lead to another Scottish referendum and, if so, the result is anyone's guess. The one certain lesson is that referendums have unpredictable consequences.

REFERENCES

Asthana, A. 2016. "No Staying in the EU by the Back Door, Says Theresa May". *The Guardian* (31 August). Retrieved from www.theguardian.com/politics/2016/

aug/31/no-staying-in-eu-by-back-door-theresa-may-brexit (accessed 30 December 2016).

BBC 2016. "Brexit: Theresa May to Trigger Article 50 by End of March". *BBC News* (2 October). Retrieved from www.bbc.co.uk/news/uk-politics-37532364 (accessed 30 December 2016).

Chang, H.-J. 2010. *Things They Don't Tell You About Capitalism.* London: Penguin.

Curtice, J. 2014. "So Who Voted Yes and Who Voted No?". 26 September. Retrieved from http://blog.whatscotlandthinks.org/2014/09/voted-yes-voted (accessed 30 December 2016).

European Commission 2016. *European Commission Directorate-General for Research and Innovation: Associated Countries.* Brussels: European Commission. Retrieved from http://ec.europa.eu/research/participants/data/ref/h2020/grants_manual/hi/3cpart/h2020-hi-list-ac_en.pdf (accessed 30 December 2016).

Gallagher, J. 2016. *Britain after Brexit: Toxic Referendums and Territorial Constitutions.* Working Paper. Oxford: Gwilym Gibbon Centre for Public Policy. Retrieved from http://ggcpp.nuff.ox.ac.uk/wp-content/uploads/2016/10/Britain-after-Brexit-Toxic-Referendums-and-Territorial-Constitutions.pdf (accessed 30 December 2016).

Gallagher, J. 2017. *Conventional Wisdom: Brexit, Devolution and the Sewel Convention.* Working Paper. Oxford: Gwilym Gibbon Centre for Public Policy. Retrieved from ggcpp.nuff.ox.ac.uk/wp-content/uploads/2017/02/Conventional-wisdom-Brexit-Devolution-and-the-Sewel-Convention.pdf (accessed 16 February 2017).

HM Government 2017. *The United Kingdom's Exit from and New Partnership with the European Union.* London: HMSO.

HM Treasury 2016. *HM Treasury Analysis: The Immediate Economic Impact of Leaving the EU.* London: HM Treasury. Retrieved from www.gov.uk/government/publications/hm-treasury-analysis-the-immediate-economic-impact-of-leaving-the-eu (accessed 30 December 2016).

Keating, M. 2016. "Can Scotland and Northern Ireland Stay in the Single Market?". 17 October. Retrieved from www.centreonconstitutionalchange.ac.uk/blog/can-scotland-and-northern-ireland-stay-single-market (accessed 30 December 2016).

Lochhead, R. 2009. "The Scottish Government's Response to the European Commission's Green Paper on Reform of the Common Fisheries Policy: Ministerial Foreword". Retrieved from www.gov.scot/Publications/2009/12/21104310/1 (accessed 30 December 2016).

McLean, I. & J. Gallagher 2016. *Future of the Land Border with the Republic of Ireland.* Working Paper. Oxford: Gwilym Gibbon Centre for Public Policy. Retrieved from http://data.parliament.uk/writtenevidence/committeeevidence.svc/evidencedocument/northern-ireland-affairs-committee/future-of-the-land-border-with-the-republic-of-ireland/written/41593.pdf (accessed 30 December 2016).

Scottish Government 2013. *Scotland's Future: Your Guide to an Independent Scotland.* Edinburgh: Scottish Government.

Scottish Government 2016. *Scotland's Place in Europe*. Edinburgh: The Scottish Government.

Smith, M. 2016. "Scots Don't Support a Second Independence Referendum". 1 September. Retrieved from https://yougov.co.uk/news/2016/09/01/davidson-now-more-popular-sturgeon-scotland (accessed 30 December 2016).

Sturgeon, N. 2016. "Nicola Sturgeon Opening Address to #SNP16". 13 October. Retrieved from www.snp.org/nicola_sturgeon_opening_address_2016 (accessed 30 December 2016).

Wright, O. 2016. "EU Referendum: Britain Will Act like Bosnia and Ukraine in Event of Brexit, Says Michael Gove". *The Independent* (19 April). Retrieved from www.independent.co.uk/news/uk/politics/eu-referendum-britain-will-act-like-bosnia-and-ukraine-in-event-of-brexit-says-michael-gove-a6991711.html (accessed 30 December 2016).

CHAPTER 8

STALLING OR BREAKING? NORTHERN IRELAND'S ECONOMY IN THE BALANCE

Leslie Budd

> ... as we know, there are known knowns; there are things we know
> we know. We also know there are known unknowns; that is to say
> we know there are some things we do not know. But there are also
> unknown unknowns – the ones we don't know we don't know.
> Donald Rumsfeld (then US Secretary of Defense),
> 12 February 2002

Actually, Rumsfeld was talking about different types of risk and uncertainty; the former being a process of assigning probabilities and the latter an environment in which no probabilities can be assigned. At present, Brexit is in the realm between "unknown unknowns" and "known unknowns" in respect of its possible outcomes. Statements by the UK prime minister to the effect that the UK will invoke Article 50 of the Lisbon Treaty that triggers the start of the two-year exit process in early 2017[1] notwithstanding, it is unclear what the outcomes will be or the time it will take to complete. Of the alternative trade scenarios, that may configure post-Brexit, most alternatives to EU membership appear difficult and challenging for the UK economy and its constituent regions and devolved nations.

In respect of the duration of these changes, one is reminded of former Chinese Premier Zhou Enlai's comment on the impact of the French Revolution that "it was too early to tell". The great unravelling of the global economy following the Global Financial Crisis (GFC) having not yet abated, in combination with the great uncoupling of Brexit, compounds these uncertainties. The multi-dimensional and multi-scalar nature of the great uncoupling means that its impact varies across the UK and the rest of the EU. In the case of the UK, the challenges are at their most sharp and complex for

---

1. And indeed the vote by the House of Commons that this will be by the end of March 2017.

Northern Ireland and its economy. The purpose of this chapter is to analyse the impact of Brexit on the Northern Ireland economy and the progress of its development as an internationally focused region.

This chapter examines the recent performance of the Northern Ireland economy, its relative performance to the UK and in comparison to that of the Republic of Ireland (ROI). Foreign Direct Investment (FDI) performance and the role of global value chains (GVCs)[2] within an all-Ireland single market are a critical element of the analysis. One of the locational parameters of FDI is the level of UK government expenditure support for the economy under the auspices of the Barnett formula.[3] Simultaneously, the level and rate of corporation tax (CT) is deemed to constrain or stimulate FDI. The proposal to devolve CT powers in Northern Ireland, with a new rate to be set at 12.5 per cent from April 2018, is now likely to have a negative effect on the economy, following Brexit. This change is briefly examined as it leads into the discussion of the challenges of Brexit for economic citizenship and governance in Northern Ireland.

I will analyse briefly the cross-border relationships with the ROI, and include estimates of the impact on the NI economy as a result of any changes to the complex border question. This subsection concludes by considering whether the different economic dimensions to Brexit can be viewed from the perspective of the theory of clubs. The original formulation of this theory relates to its application in examining public goods (Buchanan 1963). It was later applied to urban agglomerations and then to the prospects for a single currency regime in the EU (Evans 1972; Casella & Frey 1992). The announcement by the UK prime minister that the government will pursue a "hard" Brexit, in the form of almost total disengagement from the EU, suggests that there are various clubs on offer to the UK, particularly different trade models. In the case of Northern Ireland, there is an extra club that may be on offer given its special position within the UK and with respect to the Republic of Ireland.

The sophistry that the UK and particularly Northern Ireland could negotiate a free pass on trade and FDI with the other EU member states completely overlooks the complexities and timing of any changes. The fundamental constitutional and economic rub in all the Brexit noise is the border question in the island of Ireland. Effectively the maintenance of the de facto single market

---

2. The term "global value chain" describes how different stages of the production process are located across different countries. According to OECD (2015), globalization "motivates companies to restructure their operations internationally through outsourcing and offshoring of activities". For more detailed analysis, see Bailey & De Propris (2014).

3. The Barnett formula is the process by which the UK allocates government expenditure to the devolved nations of Northern Ireland, Scotland and Wales (see Keep 2015).

in all of Ireland will be undermined by proposals to constrain movement that is part of the common travel area. Consequently, transactions costs (the costs of doing business) will rise for economic agents on both sides of the border to the detriment of the performance in both economies. Indeed the political uncertainty that led to new Assembly elections in March 2017, was exacerbated by the border question after Brexit.

The fundamental question of this chapter is whether and how the impact of the great uncoupling on the currently stalling Northern Ireland economy could lead it to break from the rest of the UK in order to sustain the progress of its economic development.

CONTEXT OF THE CHARACTERISTICS OF THE NORTHERN IRELAND ECONOMY

The political economy of Northern Ireland is complex and intriguing. One could say that it punches above its weight politically given the context and conjuncture of its history within the UK. On the other hand, it punches below its weight economically given its special geographical position sharing a border with one of the EU's most dynamic economies over the last few decades. Figure 8.1 shows the relative performance of gross domestic product (GDP) for Scotland, ROI and UK against the Northern Ireland Composite Economic Indicator (NICEI). The latter acts as a proxy for GDP, with the NICEI operating at 92 per cent of pre-GFC levels.

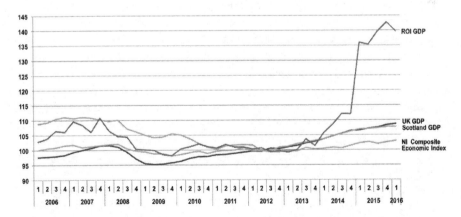

Figure 8.1 Comparison of Northern Ireland composite economic indicator and GDP for Scotland, Republic of Ireland and UK, 2006 to Q1 of 2016 (2012 = 100).

Source: Department of Economy, Northern Ireland (2016)

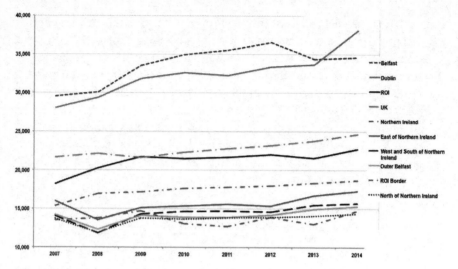

Figure 8.2 Gross value added per head Northern Ireland and sub-regions, Republic of Ireland and selected sub-regions, UK, 2007–14 (sterling, current prices).

Sources: ONS (2016); An Phríomh-Oifig Staidrimh (2016).

The sub-regional distribution is shown in Figure 8.2 that compares all the sub-regions in Northern Ireland with that of the UK, the ROI and its border region as well as Dublin. The comparison between the two main cities, Dublin and Belfast, and the border areas abutting the national territories is instructive. The two largest cities boost the relative performance of NI and ROI while the border regions of NI are more economically active than that of the ROI. This is partly a function of the relative size of the two economies, a legacy of the Troubles[4] but also the spatial distribution of sectors that tend be located in the larger number of urban centres in the ROI. The NI trend rate of growth tends to lag that of the UK by about a third, similarly the unemployment rate tends to be historically higher than the rest of the UK but tracks the trend as can be seen in Figure 8.3 below.

Similarly economic activity rates tend to be consistently lower within the 18–24 age group over time in Northern Ireland than the rest of the UK. It is notable that among the population aged 16–17, fewer women are economically inactive than men. For the 25–49 and 50–64 age groups women have

---

4. The term "The Troubles" refers to the period in Northern Ireland's history from 1968 to 1998 in which violence erupted over the political discrimination against the Catholic/Nationalist community by the Protestant/Unionist government. At the heart of the conflict was the constitutional issue of the Unionist and overwhelmingly Protestant majority wishing to remain part of the United Kingdom. The goal of the Nationalist and Republican (almost exclusively Catholic) minority was to become part of the Republic of Ireland.

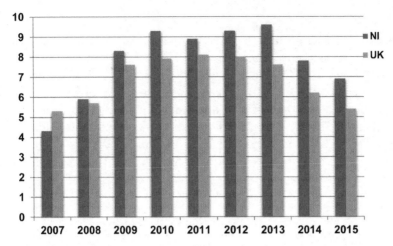

Figure 8.3 ILO unemployment rate for Northern Ireland and the UK, 2007–15 (percentage).

Source: ONS (2016).

much higher levels of economic inactivity then men. NI also has the lowest proportion of NEETs ("not in education, employment or training") in the whole of the UK, but in the 24–30 age group the proportions revert to the UK average.

The average figures for all and 18–24 cohorts are shown in Table 8.1. One of the major challenges in NI is the low level of training and skills within the younger cohort in employment. Low wages, skills and investment are seen as the main causes of internationally comparatively poor productivity performance of the UK (Riley & Rosazza Bonibene 2015). NI is one of the poorest regional performers at 14 per cent below the UK average in 2015 (Johnston & Buchanan 2016). Given its current greater economic vulnerability and the increased uncertainty that has arisen from the Brexit vote, the outlook for increased productivity in NI is weak. This is compounded by any uncertainty about its trade relationship with the ROI.

Table 8.1 Economic activity rates in Northern Ireland and the UK (all and 18–24 cohorts), 2007–15.

Cohort	2007	2008	2009	2010	2011	2012	2013	2014	2015
NI all	71.3	71.2	69.2	71.2	72.7	72.7	72.4	72.8	72.7
UK all	76.8	77.1	76.8	76.6	76.7	77.2	77.6	77.8	78.0
NI 18–24	70.4	70.5	70.6	69.8	69.8	69.7	70.1	69.8	69.6
UK 18–24	73.7	73.3	71.3	70.7	70.2	71.1	70.9	70.5	71.2

Source: ONS (2016)

The UK is the ROI's largest export market with 17 per cent of its total by value. The data for ROI trade in goods is shown in Table 8.2 below. The all-Ireland cross-border trade position (that includes services) is shown in Figure 8.4 with the UK being the largest destination for ROI exports, averaging 17 per cent of the total. It is apparent that the lack of a "hard" border facilitates trade at a lower transactions cost. The strong historical links and the peace dividend from the 1998 Good Friday Agreement in effect have created a single all-Ireland market, exchange rate differences, not withstanding. These differences also create economic arbitrage opportunities for both sets of citizens.

Table 8.2 Republic of Ireland trade in goods 2010–15 (euro millions).

Year	Northern Ireland		Great Britain		Other EU	
	Exports	*Imports*	*Export*	*Imports*	*Exports*	*Imports*
2010	1,326	990	12,677	13,823	38,640	15,300
2011	1,422	1,047	12,973	15,638	39,505	16,193
2012	1,436	1,026	13,731	15,403	39,494	17,378
2013	1,478	1,016	12,794	15,870	36,753	17,917
2014	1,605	1,104	12,137	16,461	37,193	20,896
2015	1,744	1,091	13,786	16,897	44,276	24,215

Source: An Phríomh-Oifig Staidrimh (2016).

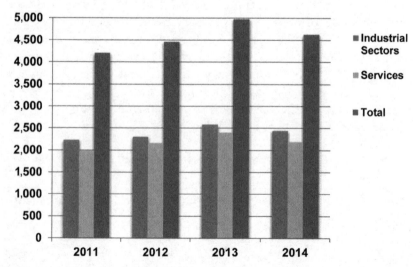

Figure 8.4 Cross-border trade, 2011–14 (sterling millions).
Source: InterTrade Ireland (2016)

Access to the wider Single European Market (SEM) has generated trade gains, leading to increased FDI, productivity and growth than otherwise would have been the case (Northern Ireland Executive 2012). The crucial importance of access to SEM is shown in Figure 8.5.

Although world trade has declined over the last few years as the great unravelling of the global economy has persisted, with a consequent decline in the EU's total share, the relative share of intra-EU trade, however, has increased (IMF 2015). This is partly due to more EU focused changes in global production networks driven by shorter GVCs. Given that 57 per cent of EU trade is intra-firm, GVCs provide the fulcrum that connects trade and FDI; both crucial elements in the NI and ROI economies. The consequences of a post-Brexit world are highly likely to be damaging given the special circumstances of NI within the UK.

The role of trade GVCs and FDI in regional economic development provides the analytical traction for investigating the impact of Brexit on the economic governance and citizenship in Northern Ireland. Edgar Morgenroth has dealt with trade in more detail in Chapter 2 of this volume, as do David Bailey and Lisa De Propris in Chapter 4, on the relationship between FDI and GVCs in the automotive sector. These issues are picked up in the next section of this chapter, the evidence of which demonstrates that the attractiveness of an economy for FDI enhances economic citizenship and governance (Donnelly 2014). One way of addressing this challenge is to draw on the economic theory of clubs to investigate what clubs are on offer to NI (and by implication to the ROI) in the different post-Brexit proposals.

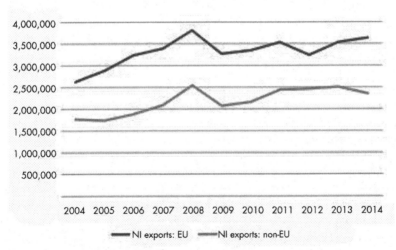

Figure 8.5 NI Exports to EU and Non-EU countries 2004–14 (sterling thousands). Source: HMRC (2015).

THE CHALLENGES OF BREXIT FOR ECONOMIC CITIZENSHIP AND GOVERNANCE

While the immediate post-Brexit economic Armageddon never occurred – and one that no respectable economist had predicted anyway – there is no counterfactual to the Bank of England loosening monetary policy further and the new Chancellor of the Exchequer signalling fiscal easing. This policy mitigation is reinforced by the UK still remaining a member state of the EU until the great uncoupling is completed. The greater uncertainty following the UK's EU membership referendum vote has had direct economic consequences in the form of delayed investment decisions and a run on sterling to its lowest level in 168 years. These impacts can be seen in Table 8.3, which shows the forecast before the Referendum compared to those adjusted for the impacts of the vote.

Table 8.3 provides some evidence that the socio-economic welfare of the citizens of NI are being disproportionately affected unless there is some extra support for its economy, given the substantial uncertainties surrounding Brexit. This outcome gets to the nub of economic citizenship and governance.

The economic role of the state can be theorized in accordance with *The Theory of the Multiple Household* (Musgrave & Musgrave 1959). The authors distinguish three branches of government:

- *allocation:* the use of fiscal instruments to secure adjustments in the allocation of resources between private and public goods;
- *distribution:* the use of fiscal instruments to secure proper adjustments in the distribution of income and wealth; and
- *stabilization:* the use of fiscal instruments to secure economic stability and growth (otherwise known as macroeconomic policy).

Table 8.3 Gross domestic product annual growth rates for Northern Ireland, UK and Republic of Ireland, 2014–18 (percentages; vote adjustments in parentheses).

2014			2015			2016			2017			2018		
NI	UK	ROI	NI	UK	ROI	NI	UK	ROI	NI	UK	ROI	NI	UK	ROI
2.8	2.4	7.1	2.9	2.2	6.7	2.6	2.6	7.2	1.8	2.7	7.7	1.5	2.5	8.6
(2.2)	(2.9)	(6.0)	(1.5)	(2.3)	(7.8)*	(1.2)	(1.8)	(4.5)	(0.3)	(0.7)	(3.3)	(0.5)	(1.1)	(4.0)

* This figure is a revised estimate following the claim by the CSO that readjusted the measure of investment in increased GDP by 26 per cent in 2015. Paul Krugman termed this adjustment "leprechaun economics".

Sources: ONS (2016); PwC NI (2016); An Phríomh-Oifig Staidrimh (2016)

The size of the expenditures advanced and the distribution between the three branches has a direct impact upon the socio-economic welfare of citizens. We can therefore advance the idea of enhanced socio-economic welfare that encompasses all citizens as a starting point for defining economic citizenship. Similarly, the governance of the three branches also has a direct impact on the utility of economic citizenship.

According to the Oates theorem, "In multilevel governments, each level of government (including the central government) will maximise social and economic welfare within its own jurisdiction" (Oates 1993: 4). The underlying logic of this theorem is that federal systems of governance create greater growth and equality, that is supported by other evidence (Martinez-Vazquez & McNab 2003; Baskaran & Feld 2013). The Global economic institutions like the International Monetary Fund (IMF) and Organisation for Economic Co-Operation and Development (OECD) also recognize that equality enhances growth as a larger total social product is created (Cingano 2014; Ostry *et al*. 2014). The essential governance challenge for Northern Ireland with respect to Brexit can be summarized as:

> An important background to the development challenges facing Northern Ireland is that the much larger Irish economy has been able to use its available policy autonomy to reap many, but not all, of the economic benefits of its sovereignty while playing a role in the wider EU system into which it is now integrated. Northern Ireland, a region of the UK with a relatively new and complicated power sharing administration, has found it more difficult to follow this policy route, either through its intra-UK links with the British economy and its regions or through its close geographical proximity and evolving links to the Irish economy, its main export market after external sales to Britain. (Bradley 2015: 3)

With regard to the three branches of government, Northern Ireland's position cuts across them in that it is part of a multilevel governance system within the UK. It also receives significant funding from the EU and resources from its immediate neighbour, the ROI, as a result of cross-border economic cooperation. The governance of this arrangement is set out in Figure 8.6 below. It is apparent that the potential loss of this significant part of this form of economic governance will damage the economic citizenship of Northern Ireland.

Underlying this process of governance is the expected impact upon two key components: FDI and GVCs: the latter being a proxy for cross-border trade and its wider UK and EU ramifications.

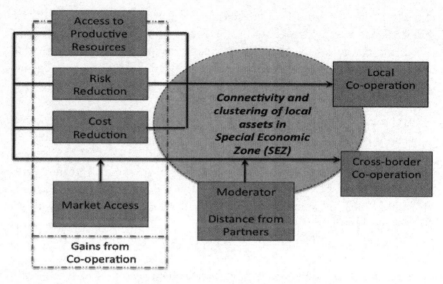

Figure 8.6 Structural relationships within cross-border governance.

Source: Roper (2006)

Estimates of the impact of Brexit in the Northern Ireland economy

Before the Referendum in June 2016, there was little specific analysis of the direct impact of Brexit on Northern Ireland. A briefing note written for the Committee of Enterprise Trade and Investment (CETI) at the Northern Ireland Assembly estimated a loss of GDP of 3 per cent directly attributable to loss of FDI; a reduction of intra-firm trade and cross-border co-operation; and, a loss of EU funding (see Budd 2015).

Oxford Economics produced a report that suggested that in the worst case scenario GDP would be 6 per cent lower by 2030 and at best, remain unchanged (Oxford Economics 2016). The CETI briefing note advised on the following direct impacts:

- *Trade and cross-border trade.* The EU accounts for 58 per cent of direct NI exports, with 37 per cent going to the ROI. As a result of Brexit, the direct and transactions costs of cross-border and economic co-operation would rise significantly. In regard to international air routes to EU and other international destinations, air fares could rise by the order of 20-30 per cent for NI departing passengers and freight. The major ROI airports would then be the more favourable destinations compared to those in NI. This issue also is part of the impact on FDI in NI.

- *Foreign direct investment.* With a potential loss of direct access to the SEM and no longer being a member of the EU's customs union, the potential loss of FDI to the ROI could be very large. Given the role of GVCs in FDI in the whole of Ireland's single market, the downstream effects and those for intermediary suppliers and small businesses would also be significant. This would bear heavily on the high value-added MATRIX sectors (telecommunications & ICT; life & health sciences; agrifood; advanced materials; advanced engineering) identified by the executive in the NI economic strategy as the key sectors to further develop and sustain the economy (Northern Ireland Executive 2012). Agri-business and aerospace in NI are particularly vulnerable to limited access to the EU, as well as the ROI being a significant FDI location in telecomms and ICT (for the impact on agribusiness see RAIS 2016).
- *Corporation tax.* From 1 April 2018, Northern Ireland will receive devolved powers to set CT, with a rate of 12.5 per cent proposed, the same as in the ROI. As a consequence NI will receive an estimated £500 million to £700 million per annum less in budgetary transfers from the UK government under the Barnett formula (Holtham Commission 2010). Combined with the loss of EU funding of £500 million per annum, this is a significant first order hit for the NI economy. Without access to the SEM and/or remaining in the EU customs union, the logic of harmonized CT rates with the ROI is undermined as the transaction costs of FDI locating in NI increase significantly. Moreover, many policy-makers in NI believe cutting CT is the "silver bullet" in transforming the economy. This follows the popular political discourse in the South, but evidence shows that the sustained economic performance in the ROI began with its accession to the SEM in 1993 (Shaxson 2012). The CETI Report *Opportunities for Excellence: The Report on the Committee's Inquiry into Growing the Economy and Providing Jobs with Lower Corporation Tax* contains an excellent and comprehensive analysis of future challenges for NI economy in respect of changes to CT (CETI 2016). CT accounts for just under 2 per cent of the total tax take in NI whose annual GDP is roughly £28 billion, so unless NI becomes the location of choice for FDI in post-Brexit UK, then this policy change will be ineffective in creating opportunities for excellence in the NI economy (for a comprehensive analysis of the CT issue; see Budd 2016).
- *EU funding.* It is apparent that the performance of the NI economy has been underpinned by funding support from the EU. Under the last programming period (2007–13), support accounted for about 8.4 per cent of GDP across a range of activities of which nearly two-thirds is accounted for by agriculture and fisheries, a key part of the agri-food sector that accounts for around 3.5 per cent of annual gross value added (GVA) and

6 per cent of employment. The loss of annual EU support funding of about £500 million per annum (about one-third of total annual GVA) would have a significant impact of the contribution of this sector to the NI economy. The programme for the 2014–20 period is central to the NI economic and innovation strategies and the achievement of the objectives within them. This funding stream also further integrates the Northern Ireland economy with others in the EU and also allows a greater degree of discretion over its own development, particularly with regard to underpinning cross-border economic cooperation and growth in FDI. In the event of Brexit, these funding streams would no longer be available. This is compounded by the loss of the net contribution of EU research and development funding to research organizations and universities in NI. For cross-funding to attract inward investment, every £1 of funding for NI Invest £2 is matched by the IDA Ireland.[5] In the event of Brexit, the IDA contribution is likely to end.

The other significant challenge is that of utility costs in NI, that for electricity generation are the highest in the UK. There is an all-Ireland market, but costs vary according to different distributors and the size of the local markets they serve. NI does import electricity from the ROI but the current capacity of the inter-connectors is insufficient to meet all demand at peak time from this cross-border supply (CETI 2014). The uncertainty over the Brexit settlement for NI suggests that cheaper energy costs will not result in the short to medium term. Longer-term questions over the sources of energy generation (renewables, etc.) ironically appear to be tied to the EU energy market, for which there is strong impetus for harmonization.

All these factors provide the locus of the border question and changes that would impact on economic citizenship and governance as a result of Brexit. To date, the focus has been whether a physical border can be reinstated between the north and south of Ireland. Some have suggested that some digital means could be used to monitor movements of goods and labour across the border, as though some form of electronic tagging could be imposed on non-UK and ROI citizens and their access to goods and services (FitzGerald & Honohan 2016). The constitutional situation has relevance for the free flow of people in that citizens of Northern Ireland are entitled to ROI passports and ROI citizens have access to UK citizenship rights. In other words, free movement of all Irish people across an EU member state and devolved nation of a former EU one, following Brexit is enshrined in UK law prior to the establishment of what has become the EU. Consequently, NI is *and*

---

5. These are the respective inward investment agencies for NI and ROI.

will remain a special case. The constitutional and then economic issue is what will be the status of migrants from the rest of the UK and other citizens from the rest of the EU who are not entitled to an ROI passport in NI, post-Brexit?

It is estimated that the 2004 wave of immigration from the Eastern European member states increased GVA by £1.2 billion and created 40,000 jobs up to 2008. Extrapolating from the downturn in growth rates following the GFC, labour market adjustment and net migrant flows, a conservative estimate would suggest that these figures increased to £3.2 billion and 55,000 jobs up until 2015. Whatever the merits of this evidence and its underlying analysis and arguments, the special status of NI arising from the combination of cross-border trade and economic co-operation, FDI, CT changes and EU funding mean the all-Ireland single market and customs union will be almost impossible to replace unless there are significantly large compensatory fiscal transfers by the UK to NI in the first part and possibly the ROI in the second. Furthermore, the transactions costs of policing and regulating intra-firm and inter-firm trade (the movement of goods and services, locational decisions of firms, capital and labour) exacerbated by increasing uncertainty will be huge. This conclusion equally applies to the ROI, whose government is seeking to insure against any damaging spillovers through increased support from other EU member states, the EC and the ECB as a member of the Eurozone. It is then axiomatic that the various models being offered for a post-Brexit UK will not be appropriate to Northern Ireland, undermining the claim to a whole UK Brexit settlement.

Brexit as a club good

Estimating the impact of Brexit on Northern Ireland is difficult in the sense that the various models being proposed are UK-wide. Yet the constitution of the UK and the composition of its economic space are complex. One way to consider assessing the impacts of different models is to view Brexit as a club good.

The theory of club goods is derived from the work of James Buchanan, the US economist who developed a theory of co-operative membership for access to shared collective goods and services (sometimes known as quasi-public and merit goods). Unlike public goods, club goods are non-rival in consumption but excludable. That is, one has to have club membership to access them, while non-members are excluded. Buchanan gives this example of a swimming pool facility:

> As more persons are allowed to share in the enjoyment of the facility, of given size, the benefit evaluation that the individual places on the good will, after some point, decline. There may, of course, be both an increasing and a constant range of the total benefit function, but at some point congestion will set in, and his evaluation of the good will fall. (Buchanan 1963: 12)

As more people join the club the costs of membership decline but so does the enjoyment of the facility as congestion approaches. Thus there is an optimal size where the cost of access equals the cost of restricting membership.

A relevant example here is the analysis of the EU common currency as a club good by Casella and Frey (1992). In their exposition they draw on the role of fiscal federalism in underpinning the prospect for a European currency union. That is, the system of fiscal transfers to compensate for the different economic capacities and capabilities of different nations and regions. The wider union then takes up the threefold functions of government expressed in *The Theory of the Multiple Household* (Musgrave & Musgrave 1959) in order to sustain the socio-economic accountability and legitimacy of this larger economic entity. Fiscal federalism based upon principles of subsidiarity (devolution of powers to the lowest level of government where appropriate) becomes a club good in that its transfers create benefits for members they would not have outside an economic union. Increases in the size of the club entail increases in the limits before congestion sets in. In the case of Brexit the new forms of membership appear to lower benefits and reduce the size at which congestion sets in.

There are four main post-Brexit clubs being offered to UK citizens, other than remaining in the current EU membership club good. The current Brexit clubs are set out in Table 8.4, based on recent work by the NI Assembly (Stennett 2016). It is apparent that only two club goods are appropriate for NI, given its special position: either the current one, inside a possibly reformed EU, or EEA membership with customs union membership included. The other alternatives would actually lead to lower benefits with congestion being reached within a variety of bilateral UK trade agreements under World Trade Organization (WTO) rules. Whether the UK could successfully negotiate its own version of CETA is uncertain and the negotiation itself could be of long duration, increasing transactions costs for both economies in Ireland. There could be the possibility of a particular club good, such as the cross-border club, that maintains the effective status quo for NI and the ROI, for which there is an economic rationale but the political barriers are likely to be high.

Table 8.4 Potential Brexit club goods.

Club good	Financial contribution	Impact from EU rules and SEM access	Influence over EU rules
Current EU	0.6% of GDP from UK in 2016 but no separate contribution from NI	Full access to SEM – no tariffs or custom duties. Trade and air route access negotiated at EU level lowering transactions costs for member state. EU-wide environmental practice. Common agricultural and fisheries policies standardizing product quality and market access. Common external tariffs to prevent anti-competitive dumping (e.g. steel).	NI represented through UK on all institutions
European Economic Area (Norway)	Contributes to EU budget equivalent to 0.34% of UK GDP (2016), but does not contribute to common agricultural policy (CAP)	Full access to SEM but EEA agreement does not cover CAP and CFP and customs union and common trade policy Matches EU rules and standards on agriculture and committed to process of liberalizing agricultural trade. Some exemptions apply to environmental regulations. Co-operation between Norway and EU in energy security and part of SEM in energy.	Right to consultation but not represented in EU institutions
European Free Trade Area (Switzerland)	No obligation for EFTA members to contribute to EU budget, but Switzerland contributes equivalent to 0.11% of UK GDP, to cover costs of participation in various programmes including research	Switzerland's agreement with EU covers movement of persons and access to SEM for a number of sectors. Passporting rights of Swiss Banks operating in EU member states. Consultative role on management of environment rules and regulations. Not covered by CAP with series of bilateral trade agreements on agricultural trade and lower customs duties. Environmental management based upon a range of sectoral agreements.	No formal right to be consulted on EU laws and regulations
Free Trade Agreement (Canada and the EU)	The Comprehensive Economic and Trade Agreement (CETA) between Canada has been agreed and ratified but no financial contribution	CETA gives Canada almost complete access to the SEM with the exception of financial and other services. Joint environmental and climate protection but concerns over GM product and carbon heavy fuels that are not included. Up to 94% of agricultural exports from Canada will be tariff-free. Tariff-free changes to some fisheries product but food safety and labelling missing from agreement.	No formal right to influence EU policies
WTO	None	EU is member of WTO with UK having to negotiate separate membership post-Brexit. WTO exporters to EU have to comply with environmental regulations to access SEM. For countries with WTO Most Favoured Nation (MFN) status the average tariff is 5.4% but average agricultural tariff is 12.2%. Complex set of arrangements covering 6526 tariffs including fisheries. No WTO rules in services.	No formal powers

Source: Stennett (2016)

CONCLUSION: SLOW STALLING OR BREAKING BAD

The NI economy was beginning to stall before the UK's EU membership referendum, mainly due to its economy not recovering to pre-GFC levels, compounded by increased global economic uncertainty. This position was exacerbated by the austerity imposed on Northern Ireland in the form of public expenditure cuts and constraints by the UK government. The devaluation of sterling to historic lows after the Brexit vote increased the value of EU agricultural subsidies in NI, but Brexit will end these payments. Uncertainty over which form of Brexit club good will be available not only for the UK but also its constituent nations has also contributed to a significant slowing of the NI economy. The logic of devolving corporation tax has now been undermined by the Brexit vote given the importance of FDI that is likely to be smaller alongside its cross-border dynamics. A lower CT take will be compounded by a reduced Barnett formula budgetary settlement with the UK government. The withdrawal of EU funding is likely to significantly increase the costs to the economy of this "double whammy". It is clear that the border question is not just about one about what kind of physical controls or its constitutional aspects. The economic consequences of exiting from this form of club good of SEM access and customs union membership are also liable to be very large.

The question of whether Brexit will break the progress of the NI economy is in the realm of unknown unknowns. There are however sufficient known unknowns to suggest that the special case of NI will require it to have a specific settlement, if this outcome is to be avoided. In the television series *Breaking Bad* the central character is a financially stretched chemistry teacher resorting to manufacturing a pure version of a very popular illegal drug. He chooses Heisenberg as his drug-producing and dealing alias that attracts an almost mythical status as his reputation and scale of activity grow. Werner Heisenberg was the Nobel Prize-winning physicist who created the "uncertainty principle" that states that the position and velocity of a particle cannot both be measured, exactly, at the same time (actually pairs of position, energy and time). The application of this hypothesis is also relevant to the relationship between economic citizenship and governance in the face of external economic shocks and societal fracture. In the case of our television anti-hero, he was in the realm of known unknowns until his position eventually went bad as he delved deeper into the violent world of drug production and dealing: a world, that he was not ultimately emotionally or socially equipped to deal with.

Without a proper, specific and appropriate settlement for NI, Brexit could break bad for the whole of the UK, in undermining and fracturing the relationship between its economic citizenship and governance. The multi-level governance structures and processes in the UK then may not be equipped to deal with the consequences of Brexit, especially in Northern Ireland.

REFERENCES

An Phríomh-Oifig Staidrimh 2016. *Regional Economic Statistics*. Dublin: An Phríomh-Oifig Staidrimh/Central Statistics Office (CSO).

Bailey. D. & L. De Propris 2014. "Manufacturing Reshoring and its Limits: The UK Automotive Case". *Cambridge Journal of Regions Economy and Society* **7**(2): 379–95.

Baskaran, T. & L. P. Feld 2013. "Fiscal Decentralization and Economic Growth in OECD Countries: Is There a Relationship?". *Public Finance Review* **41**(4): 421–45.

Bradley, J. 2015. *Brexit, Northern Ireland and the Island Economy: An Update*. Dublin: Institute of International and European Affairs.

Buchanan, J. 1963. "An Economic Theory of Clubs". *Economica* **32**(125): 1–14.

Budd, L. 2015. *The Consequences for the Northern Ireland Economy if the United Kingdom Exits from the European Union*. Committee for Enterprise Trade and Investment (CETI) Briefing Note 03/15. Belfast: Northern Ireland Assembly.

Budd, L. 2016. "Economic Challenges and Opportunities of Devolved Corporate Taxation in Northern Ireland". In *Devolution and the UK Economy*, D. Bailey & L. Budd (eds), 95–114. London: Rowman & Littlefield.

Casella, A. & B. Fey 1992. "Federalism and Clubs: Towards an Economic Theory of Overlapping Political Jurisdictions". *European Economic Review* **36**: 639–46.

CETI 2014. *Report on the Committee's Review into Electricity Policy, Part 2: Electricity Pricing*. Belfast: Northern Ireland Assembly.

CETI 2016. *Opportunity for Excellence: The Report on the Committee's Inquiry into Growing the Economy and Providing Jobs with Lower Corporation Tax*. Belfast: Northern Ireland Assembly.

Cingano, F. 2014. *Trends in Income Inequality and its Impact on Economic Growth*. OECD Social, Employment and Migration Working Papers, no. 163. Paris: OECD.

Department for Economy, Northern Ireland 2016. *Economic Commentary*. March. Belfast: Northern Ireland Executive.

Donnelly, D. 2014. *A Review of Literature Regarding the Determinants of Foreign Direct Investment (FDI)*. Research and Information Service Briefing Paper NIAR 862-14. Belfast: Northern Ireland Assembly.

Evans, A. 1972. "The Pure Theory of City Size in an Industrial Economy". *Urban Studies* **9**: 49–77.

FitzGerald, J. & P. Honohan 2016. "Ireland and Brexit". In *Brexit Beckons: Thinking Ahead by Leading Economists*, R. E. Baldwin (ed.), 129–36. London: Centre for Economic Policy Research.

HMRC 2015. *Trade: Info*. London: HMRC.

Holtham Commission 2010. *Final Report*. Independent Commission on Funding and Finance for Wales (Holtham Commission). Cardiff: Government of Wales.

IMF 2015. *World Economic Outlook*. Washington, DC: International Monetary Fund.

InterTrade Ireland 2016. *International Trade Statistics*. Dublin: Intertrade Ireland.

Johnston, R. & J. Buchanan 2016. *Understanding Productivity in Northern Ireland*. Coleraine: Centre for Economic Policy, University of Ulster.

Keep, M. 2015. *The Barnett Formula*. House of Commons Library Briefing Paper no. 7836. London: House of Commons.

Martinez-Vazquez, J. & R. M. McNab 2003. "Fiscal Decentralization and Economic Growth". *World Development* **31**(9): 1597–616.

Musgrave, R. A. & P. B. Musgrave 1959. *Public Finance in Theory and Practice*. New York: McGraw-Hill.

Northern Ireland Executive 2012. *Economic Strategy Priorities for Sustainable Growth and Prosperity: Building a Better Future*. Belfast: Norther Ireland Executive.

Oates, W. E. 1993. *Fiscal Decentralization and Economic Development*. Working Paper no. 93-4. College Park, MD: University of Maryland.

OECD 2015. "Global Value Chains". Retrieved from www.oecd.org/sti/ind/global-value-chains.htm (accessed 30 December 2016).

ONS 2016. *Regional Trends*. London: Office for National Statistics.

Ostry, J. D., A. Berg & C. G. Tsangarides 2014. *Redistribution, Inequality, and Growth*. IMF Discussion Note SDN/14/92. Washington, DC: International Monetary Fund.

Oxford Economics 2016. *The Economic Implications of a UK Exit from the EU for Northern Ireland*. Briefing Paper, February. Oxford: Oxford Economics.

PwC NI 2011. "Corporation Tax: Game Changer or Game Over?" Retrieved from www.pwc.co.uk/ni/publications/ni-government-futures-corporation-tax.html (accessed 23 May 2015).

Riley, R. & C. Rosazza Bonibene 2015. *The UK Productivity Puzzle 2008–2013: Evidence From British Businesses*. National Institute for Economic and Social Research Discussion Paper no. 450. London: NIESR.

Roper, S. 2006. *Cross-Border and Local Cooperation on the Island of Ireland: An Economic Perspective*. Belfast: Centre for International Borders Research and Dublin: Institute for British-Irish Studies.

Rumsfeld, D. 2002. "DoD News Briefing – Secretary Rumsfeld and Gen. Myers". 12 February. Retrieved from http://archive.defense.gov/Transcripts/Transcript.aspx?TranscriptID=2636 (accessed 30 December 2016).

Shaxson, N. 2012. *Treasure Islands: Tax Havens and the Men who Stole the World*. London: Vintage.

Stennett, A. 2016. *The EU Referendum and Potential Implications for Northern Ireland*. Research and Information Service Research Paper NIAR 32-16. Belfast: Northern Ireland Assembly.

CHAPTER 9

BREXIT AND REGIONAL DEVELOPMENT IN THE UK: WHAT FUTURE FOR REGIONAL POLICY AFTER STRUCTURAL FUNDS?

John Bachtler

INTRODUCTION

The results of the EU referendum showed profound spatial differences in opinion across the UK. Inequality has been widely discussed as a major factor explaining these differences, with some of the highest shares of the Leave vote in areas experiencing greatest economic difficulty, especially in northern England and Wales. The UK Government appears to share this view, with the prime minister making a series of political commitments to address inequality. The new industrial policy of the renamed Department of Business, Energy and Industrial Strategy includes recognition of the "importance of place".

The question is how the rhetoric will be translated into practice. A once powerful domestic UK-wide regional policy has been largely whittled away, with divergent approaches to regional development following devolution and the disappearance of regional development institutions and instruments, superseded by local and urban initiatives with variable resources, coherence or permanence. The one policy that has been maintained over the long term will be phased out as part of Brexit. This is EU structural funds – which is currently providing an allocation of £10 billion of EU funding to the UK over the 2014–20 period.

This provides a challenge and an opportunity to the UK government and to the devolved administrations. The loss of EU structural funds significantly affects the "Less-Developed Regions" of West Wales & the Valleys, Cornwall & the Isles of Scilly, as well as in the former industrial regions that were major beneficiaries of EU funding, not least those that could have anticipated significantly more EU receipts after 2020, such as Tees Valley and Durham. While the UK government has guaranteed funding for any structural funds projects approved until the UK leaves the EU, it has not made any commitments to replacement funding for recipient regions thereafter.

Resources are not the only issue. EU cohesion policy provided stability through multi-annual programmes, promoted a strategic and integrated approach to development and required partnership-working between central and subnational levels of government. Although the technical administration of EU funding has become increasingly complex and prescriptive, its disappearance will leave a void. The UK government and devolved administrations have the challenge of deciding whether and what aspects of the EU funding regime should be retained as part of any successor policy framework.

The domestic context for future development policy-making is characterised by a complicated patchwork of territorially focused interventions. These include the devolution deals agreed or under negotiation in England, the future of the "Northern Powerhouse", the "Midlands Engine", local enterprise partnerships, enterprise zones, and the remaining regional/local growth funding. The first policy thinking on a new industrial strategy was provided in the 2016 Autumn Statement signalling more attention and investment in regional infrastructure, enterprise and productivity. Less clear is the extent to which the UK Government's policy approach to regional and local issues will be one of continuity or radical change.

Questions about territorial responses to inequality have also been asked by the devolved administrations in recent years. In Scotland, the 2016 programme for government prioritized "inclusive growth" including action to address regional economic inequalities, and the current Enterprise and Skills Review in Scotland includes consideration of the appropriate regional/local scale of future economic development intervention. The existing development strategies for Wales and Northern Ireland both recognize the need for sub-regional balance and to address specific regional and local requirements.

This chapter explores these issues in more detail. It begins by reviewing the evidence for the importance of territorial inequality in the outcome of the EU referendum, and then discusses the role and importance of EU structural funds in the UK, past and present, before considering the future of domestic approaches to regional and local development.

BREXIT AND TERRITORIAL INEQUALITY

The EU referendum showed clear divides among voters by age, education, employment and social class – and by area. While the UK as a whole voted Leave, there were sizeable majorities for Remain in Scotland, Northern Ireland, London and Gibraltar (see Table 9.1).

Table 9.1 Regional votes to Remain or Leave.

Region	Remain	Leave
England	46.8%	53.2%
Northern Ireland	55.8%	44.2%
Scotland	62.0%	38.0%
Wales	47.5%	52.5%
England's NUTS 1 regions		
South East	48.2%	51.8%
London	59.9%	40.1%
North West	46.3%	53.7%
East	43.5%	56.5%
South West	47.4%	52.6%
West Midlands	40.7%	59.3%
Yorkshire and Humberside	42.3%	57.7%
East Midlands	41.2%	58.8%
North East	42.0%	58.0%
Gibraltar	95.9%	4.1%

Source: BBC (2016)

Several initial analyses of voting patterns since the referendum have argued that territorial inequality is a major explanatory factor of the referendum outcome. In England, voting in favour of EU membership was higher in affluent areas in and around London, notably along the M4 corridor, as well as in university cities – Bristol, Manchester, Oxford, Cambridge, Norwich and York (Savage & Cunningham 2016). Those areas with lower median wages, low levels of skills, lack of opportunities and higher levels of poverty were significantly more likely to vote Leave (Bell & Machin 2016; Darvas 2016; Goodwin & Heath 2016). Goodwin (2016) concluded that "Brexit drew most of its strength from voters who have felt left behind by the rapid economic transformation of Britain, or more accurately of London and south east England".

The impact of migration may also be a factor. While large numbers of migrants in an area do not appear to be associated with a higher propensity to vote Leave (areas with the highest proportion of migrants voted predominantly Remain), the rate of change in migrant numbers seems to be influential (Becker *et al.* 2016). Carozzi (2016) finds that "places that experienced a larger relative increase in migration between 2001 and 2011 disproportionately supported leaving the EU". The town of Boston is regarded as emblematic: the town with the highest proportion of Leave voters has experienced both significant economic deprivation and a steep increase in migration from Central and Eastern Europe since 2004 (Goodwin 2016).

Economic inequality may only be part of the story. Analysis by Savage and Cunningham (2016) shows that social capital (people's social networks) is the strongest predictor of referendum voting patterns. They argue that it is entrenched unequal access to a combination of economic, social and cultural capital in a country with low intergenerational mobility that explains the maps of Leave and Remain.

The results also need to be seen in the wider political context and dynamics of the referendum. One issue is the way that the respective campaigns in the referendum utilized concerns about economic situation and migration. As Mourlon-Druol (2016) notes: "the wealth–immigration–EU link was used as a means to explain economic and social discontent". However, those receptive to this and other Leave messages were not exclusively in the more deprived areas of the UK. Many people who voted Leave were in the middle classes, lived in the Midlands and south of England (Dorling 2016), and were significantly motivated also by other factors such as national identity, values and attitudes to the EU (Ashcroft 2016; Korski 2016).

The results in Scotland and Northern Ireland – where turnouts were the lowest in the UK but both voted to remain – also indicate the importance of different factors. The influence of social divisions on voting patterns in Scotland is said to be similar to England and Wales, but "in a country where UKIP has little resonance and where a pro-European SNP has come to dominate the political landscape, views that elsewhere disinclined many a voter to back Remain had less impact north of the border" (Curtice 2016).

Clearly, the role of inequality in explanations of the referendum results needs further research. However, whatever the causal factors, policy-makers need to consider how they respond to a highly unequal country. Recent Eurostat data indicate that London has a regional GDP per head (PPS, EU28 = 100) of 186 against a national average of 109, with figures of 525 for Inner London West and 204 for Inner London East (Eurostat 2016). Darvas and Wolff (2016) have shown that the UK has the highest level of income inequality and lowest level of intergenerational social mobility in the EU. Moreover, while regional disparities in the UK are high and have increased over the past decade, they are part of a longer-standing historical problem of spatial economic imbalance (Martin et al. 2015; McCann 2016). The next sections turn to the question of policy responses, first the contribution of EU structural funds and then the post-Brexit future of regional policy in the UK.

WHAT HAVE EU STRUCTURAL FUNDS DONE FOR US?

Structural funds have been an important part of the UK regional policy environment for 40 years. The creation of the European Regional Development Fund (ERDF) in 1975 was a product of British accession to the EEC, partly to offset UK budgetary contributions and to address the major problems of industrial restructuring in the UK.

The early ERDF funding accounted for only five per cent of the EEC budget and was initially allocated under a quota system, providing funding for projects in the assisted areas of national regional policies. In the United Kingdom, which had a quota allocation of around 28 per cent of the Community total (second only to Italy), virtually all the assistance was used to co-finance projects funded by the British regional policy measures of the time, Regional Development Grant and Regional Selective Assistance, in the Special Development Areas and Development Areas. The UK continued to be eligible for an average of 20–25 per cent of the budget through the various reforms up to the mid-1980s, bringing the UK some 600 million ECU per year in the mid-1980s, equivalent to roughly £1 billion per year in 2016 prices (Vanhove 1999; Bachtler *et al.* 2013a).

When a geographical prioritization of support (based on a GDP per head threshold of 75 per cent of the EC average) was introduced in 1984, Northern Ireland was one of the "priority regions", along with southern Italy, Greece

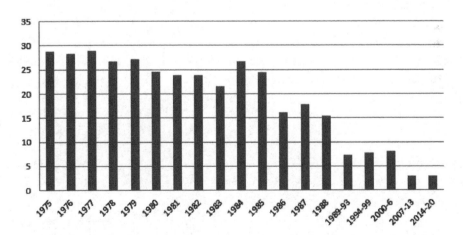

Figure 9.1 UK percentage share of EC/EU cohesion policy appropriations 1975–2020. Note: shares are for ERDF up to 1988, thereafter for all structural funds from 1989 to 2020.

Source: ERDF annual reports; Bachtler *et al.* (2006, 2013b); Mendez *et al.* (2013)

and Republic of Ireland. Scotland was another big beneficiary; during the first ten years of the ERDF (1975–84), it was the third highest recipient of Community aid (after Campania and Sicilia), receiving 6.4 per cent of all Community assistance for ERDF support measures, and worth 744 million ECU equivalent to 247 ECU per head. Other UK industrial regions – North, Midlands, Wales – were also receiving over 200 ECU per head from the ERDF. The UK was similarly to the fore when the first experimentation with a programme approach was introduced in the mid-1980s. The UK was a beneficiary of 30 per cent of the funding allocated to the new National Programmes of Community Interest, with the NPCI for Glasgow receiving the largest single EC allocation of funding (92.3 million ECU), and other substantial programmes were approved for Tayside, Mid-Glamorgan, Teesside, Birmingham and West Lothian in the 1986–7 period (European Commission 1987, 1989).

The scale and role of EC funding in this period cannot be underestimated. The 1983 Regional Development Act had significantly downgraded the profile and resources of domestic regional policy:

> Although an economic case for regional policy may still be made, it is not self-evident ... Expenditure on regional policy imposes a burden on taxpayers throughout the country through either high taxation or increased Government borrowing which crowd out other activities in the economy generally.
>
> (House of Commons 1983)

Indeed, without the need for UK co-financing of ERDF programmes, it is likely that much of the remaining regional and industrial policy intervention of the time would have been largely abolished.

Following the reform of the structural funds in 1988, cohesion policy funding was allocated to member states according to EU criteria for multiannual periods of 5–7 years. Allocations were initially based on regional eligibility:

- Objective 1: lagging regions with a GDP per head below 75 per cent of the EU average(subsequently termed Convergence and then Less-Developed Regions).
- Objective 2: industrial and restructuring regions designated principally on the basis of (un)employment criteria (later called Regional and Competitiveness and then More-Developed Regions).
- Objective 5b: regions experiencing rural underdevelopment, based on agricultural employment/income and GDP (merged with Objective 2 from 2000 onwards).

During the 1990s, over 40 per cent of the UK's population were in these designated areas – Northern Ireland, Merseyside and Highlands & Islands under Objective 1, all the old-industrial areas of Northern England, the Midlands, South Wales and Western Scotland (Objective 2), and the rural areas of Northern and Western England, Central Wales and Scotland (Objective 5b). Preparations for EU enlargement in the early 2000s led to cuts in the coverage of eligible areas in the EU15, although the UK still had almost a third of the national population in designated Objective 1 regions (Cornwall, South Yorkshire and West Wales & the Valleys) and Objective 2 areas.

From 2007 onwards, structural funds became available to all regions in the UK, but with a continued focus on the lagging (now Convergence) areas with higher rates of award and aid intensity. The all-region approach has continued into the current 2014–20 period (see Figure 9.2), though with only Cornwall & and the Isles of Scilly, West Wales & the Valleys being designated as lagging regions (now Less-Developed Regions). The temporary transitional arrangements that had characterized every previous period for dedesignated regions has now been formalized with a specific category of Transition Regions, which also have higher rates of award.

Funding flows are difficult to identify because of differences between initial allocations at the start of a funding period and the eventual outturn of expenditure; allocations in national currencies also varied in line with exchange rate changes. Nevertheless, the data in Table 9.2 below indicate that allocations to the UK structural funds over the 1989–2020 period have amounted to at least €55 billion. Given that the EU funding has needed to be co-financed with at least 25 per cent of national (public/private) funding in Objective 1 regions, and 50 per cent in other regions, the total economic development expenditure associated with structural funds in the UK over the 1989–2020 period could approach €100 billion.

Importantly, the regional distribution of EU funding in the UK ensures that poorer regions (and poorer localities) receive higher per capita shares of the structural funds (see Table 9.3). During the 2014–20 period, the highest allocations are to Wales (€788 per head), Northern Ireland (€338), North East England (€285) and South West England (€283) (SPERI 2016).

The governance of structural funds in the UK has been "dynamic", associated with more institutional change over the period since 1989 than in any other member state (see Table 9.4).

The first round of programmes for the 1989–93 period were largely drawn up in Whitehall (according to a set template for all the English programmes) and the Northern Irish, Scottish and Welsh Offices respectively but with (at least some) participation of regional and local "partnerships". For 1994–99, the programming and management of funding in England was decentral-

Figure 9.2 Structural funds areas in the United Kingdom, 2014–20.

Source: DG Regio

ized to regional Government Offices, allowing more regional specificity to be introduced – and encouraged by an activist Directorate-General (DG XVI) in the European Commission that was keen to "bypass" Whitehall control of the Funds. During the 1990s, Scotland used an innovative partnership-based model for delivering structural funds, also encouraged by DG XVI, based on programme management executives (PMEs) that were steered

Table 9.2 Estimated cohesion policy allocations to the UK, 1989–2020 (€ millions, constant prices).

Period	Regional allocations			Other funding		Total
1989–93	Objective 1 1,359	Objective 2 4,442	Objective 5b 600			6,401
1994–99	Objective 1 3,521	Objective 2 3,196	Objective 5b 1,219			7,936
2000–06	Objective 1 6,960	Objective 2 5,460		Objective 3 6,253	FIFG 166	18,839
2007–13	Convergence 3,056	Phasing/out 126	RCE 6,712	ETC 806		10,700
2014–20	LDR 2,383	Transition 2,617	MDR 5,768	ETC 865		11,633
Total						55,510

Note: the figures are based on allocations at the start of each period and may not equate to actual expenditure. RCE: Regional Competitiveness and Employment; LDR: Less-Developed Regions; MDR: More-Developed Regions; ETC: European Territorial Cooperation. FIFG: Financial Instrument for Fisheries Guidance (non-Objective 1).

Sources: Bachtler *et al.* (2013a); Inforegio (http://ec.europa.eu/regional_policy/en)

Table 9.3 Regional allocations of structural funds in the UK, 2007–13 and 2014–20.

Region	Combined ERDF and ESF allocations (€ millions) 2014–20	Per capita combined ERDF and ESF allocations 2014–20
East of England	387	66
East Midlands	598	132
London	762	93
North East	739	285
North West	1,132	161
South East	286	33
South West	1,495	283
West Midlands	909	162
Yorkshire and Humber	794	150
Scotland	895	169
Northern Ireland	513	338
Wales	2,312	788
England	6,937	131
Total	10,858	172

Source: UK Parliament House of Commons Written Answers 32053 (22.3.16) and 33071 (8.4.16); SPERI (2016) SPERI (2016)

Table 9.4 The evolving governance of structural funds (ERDF and ESF) in the United Kingdom.

Period	England	Northern Ireland	Scotland	Wales
1989–93	Department of Trade and Industry; Department of the Environment (DoE)	Department of Finance and Personnel	Scottish Office	Welsh Office
1994–99	Regional Government Offices; DoE, then Office of the Deputy Prime Minister (ODPM)	Department of Finance and Personnel	Programme. Management Executives (PMEs) – 5; Scottish Office	Welsh Office; Wales European Partnership Executive
2000–06	Regional Development Agencies; OPDM	Department of Finance and Personnel	PMEs – 5; Scottish Government	Welsh Government (Wales European Funding Office, WEFO)
2007–13	Regional Development Agencies; Department of Communities and Local Government (DCLG); Local Enterprise Partnerships	Department of Enterprise, Trade and Investment	Scottish Government; PMEs – 2	Welsh Government (WEFO)
2014–20	DCLG; Local Enterprise Partnerships	Department for the Economy	Scottish Government	Welsh Government (WEFO)

by local authorities, colleges and other sectors, although the Scottish Office was responsible for claims and payments.[1] A shorter-lived PME – the Welsh European Programme Executive – was used during this period in Wales.

1. These comprised one PME for ESF and four regional PMEs for ERDF: Strathclyde European Partnership, East of Scotland European Partnership, South of Scotland European Partnership, and Highlands & Islands Partnership Programme.

In some respects, the late 1990s and early 2002 were a more favourable period for EU funding in the UK. The incoming Labour Government used a report by former EU Commissioner Bruce Millan to redesign a regionalized institutional framework for regional policy – based around regional development agencies (RDAs) and regional strategies – that was more conducive to the programming and management of structural funds. Thus, further decentralization in England took place with the transfer of structural funds responsibilities to the RDAs for the 2000–06 period.

However, the RDAs were summarily abolished in 2010–12 in favour of re-centralized management by the UK Department of Communities & Local Government. ERDF in 2014–20 is now managed through national programmes in England with delivery at a sub-regional scale through Local Enterprise Partnerships. Following devolution to Scotland and Wales, the functions of the PMEs were progressively rationalized (reducing them from five to two in Scotland) and eventually subsumed into the devolved administrations of the Welsh Government (Welsh European Funding Office) and Scottish Government (Structural Funds Division). Northern Ireland had relatively more stability with management being undertaken by the Northern Ireland Office – Department of Finance and Personnel – until devolution after which management functions were exercised by the Department for Enterprise, Trade and Investment, renamed as the Department for the Economy.

The use of structural funds in the UK has also evolved in line with changing concepts of regional development and EU priorities. In the first 1989–93 programme period, the focus was predominantly on generic forms of business aid and infrastructure, reflecting the UK regional and industrial policy priorities of the time. As in most other member states, strategic thinking was limited, and the programmes were seen as a vehicle for drawing down EU funding. For the 1994–99 period, the Commission used new regulatory provisions to conduct its own ex ante evaluation of the UK programme proposals and encourage (or oblige) UK authorities to take more strategic approach to structural funds, including a greater focus on R&D and SME development and pioneering support for community economic development.

The 2000s saw a major shift in the use of structural funds in the UK, as elsewhere in the EU. Funding priorities became more prescriptive, initially with a requirement to focus on innovation, and from the early 2000s onwards, governed by the objectives of the Lisbon and Gothenburg strategies (growth and jobs, and sustainable development). Indeed, for 2007–13, minimum levels of spending had to be "earmarked" for Lisbon priorities, albeit formulated in general terms. The main effect was to reduce significantly spending on infrastructure and increase radically the allocations to innovation, enterprise and the green economy (see Table 9.5). In the current, 2014–20 period, the use of the Funds has been subject to still more direction from the EU level. With cohesion policy being used as a "delivery vehicle" for Europe 2020 goals (European Commission 2011), UK and other programmes have been required to allocate funding to specific thematic objectives, with minimum amounts allocated to RTDI, SME competitiveness, low-carbon and social inclusion.

A distinctive element of structural funds in the UK affected by Brexit is European Territorial Cooperation (ETC). With an EU allocation of €865 million, the UK is involved in 14 ETC programmes (see Table 9.6), primarily with neighbouring countries. Interreg programmes are one of the accepted areas of "European added value", and while the economic outcomes are sometimes difficult to evaluate, research indicates that they provide valued opportunities for regional, local and community organizations and the private sector to

Table 9.5 Division of UK financial resources for the 2007–13 period by theme, at start (2007) and closure (2016) of programme (ERDF only, € millions).

Category	2007	2016
1. Innovation & RTD	2224.2	1795.0
2. Entrepreneurship	559.0	462.6
3. Other investment in enterprise	442.7	665.4
4. ICT for citizens & business	313.1	301.6
5. Environment	350.2	405.4
6. Energy	280.6	330.8
7. Broadband	85.5	266.3
8. Road	59.0	253.1
9. Rail	62.9	65.4
10. Other transport	246.4	169.5
11. Human capital	4.0	4.0
12. Labour market	48.3	28.9
13. Culture and social infrastructure	71.1	73.3
14. Social inclusion	41.0	10.1
15. Territorial dimension	456.2	451.8
16. Capacity building	2.0	2.0
17. Technical assistance	169.8	101.6
Total	5416.0	5386.9

Source: Applica and Ismeri Europa (2016)

Table 9.6 European Territorial Programmes 2014–20 with UK involvement.

Programme	Area	Allocation (€ millions)
Two Seas	South West, South East and East of England, coastal parts of France (Channel, North Sea), Flanders and Netherlands	257
Interreg VA France–England	South West, South East and East of England and Finisterre to Pas-de-Calais in France	223
Interreg VA Ireland–N. Ireland–Scotland	South Western Scotland, Highlands & Islands, Northern Ireland, and Border Midlands Western region of Ireland	240
Interreg VA Ireland–Wales	West Wales and the Valleys, East Wales and Southern and Eastern region of Ireland	79
Northern Periphery and Arctic	Highlands and Islands, Northern Ireland, Western and Northern parts of Ireland, Norway, Sweden and Finland, and Faroe Islands, Greenland, Iceland and Canada	50
North Sea	Eastern parts of the UK, Norway and Denmark, parts of Flanders, North Western Germany, North Western Netherlands and South Western Sweden	167
Atlantic Area	Western parts of England and Wales, Ireland, Portugal, Northern Ireland, Scotland, France and Spain	140
Ireland–UK PEACE IV	Northern Ireland and Border Midland Western region of Ireland	229
North West Europe	Whole of the UK, Ireland, Belgium, Luxembourg, Switzerland and most of Germany, Netherlands and Northern France	396
South West Europe	Gibraltar, Portugal, Spain and South-west France	107
Interreg Europe	all EU member states, plus Norway and Switzerland	359
INTERACT, URBACT, ESPON 2020	Research, information exchange and best-practice sharing for all EU countries (INTERACT), plus Norway and Switzerland (URBACT) plus Iceland and Liechtenstein (ESPON 2020)	159

Source: Department of Business, Energy and Industrial Strategy

develop joint projects on common areas of interest, as well as providing an international dimension to regional and local development thinking and practice (Mirwaldt & McMaster 2008; Hörnström 2012; ADE 2016).

Looking forward, if the UK had voted to stay in the EU, the country could well have claimed a larger proportion of the cohesion policy budget after 2020 given the relatively poorer performance of UK regions in an EU context in recent years. Over the 2008–14 period, Eurostat data show a decline in regional GDP per head (PPS) as a percentage of the EU28 in every NUTS region in the UK with the exception of Inner and Outer London (which increased) and Cumbria, Herefordshire, Worcestershire and Warwickshire, and West Wales & the Valleys (which stayed static).

This would imply significant shifts in the eligibility status of UK regions for structural funds (see Table 9.6). A comparison of eligibility at the start of the current 2014–20 period and the equivalent based on the latest data shows that nine regions (with a population of 16.2 million people) would move downwards into a lower category of eligibility: eight of them would be redesignated from More-Developed Region (MDR) status to be Transition Regions, and one (Tees Valley and Durham) would become a Less-Developed Region (LDR). Three regions have improved relative to the EU average sufficiently to have a higher eligibility status: Cumbria and the Highlands & Islands would move from Transition Region to MDR region status; and Cornwall & the Isles of Scilly would move out of the LDR category.

While the scale, governance and use of structural funds in the UK are clear, the effectiveness of the funding is more contested. The UK structural funds programmes are very small compared to the size of the UK economy, making up only around 0.1 per cent of UK GDP (HM Government 2012). Consequently, the overall impact of structural funds spending has been minor. However, the relative importance of structural funds resources as a proportion of regional GVA varies widely: those regions in the highest category of eligibility (currently Cornwall, Isles of Scilly, West Wales and the Valleys, previously South Yorkshire, Merseyside, Northern Ireland and the Highlands & Islands) and some old-industrial regions have gained much higher amounts of ERDF investment per capita or unit of GVA (Regeneris 2013).

Ex post evaluations have been undertaken by the European Commission at the end of each programme period. Evaluations of ERDF for the most recent programme periods (2000–06 and 2007–13) found that structural funds interventions in the UK were associated with significant numbers of new and safeguarded jobs, land redevelopment, increases in SME turnover, innovation projects, training and skills development, the creation of community enterprises and other results (Applica et al. 2009; Applica & Ismeri Europa 2016).

Specifically, for the 2007–13 period, Applica and Ismeri Europa (2016) concluded that ERDF support up to end of 2014 led directly to the creation of over 152,000 jobs, over 29,000 of them in SMEs and around 3,800 in research (see Table 9.8). These were the result, in part, of the support to almost 1,800 RTD projects and over 7,300 cooperation projects between enterprises and research institutes, while over 52,700 businesses were helped to start up. Additional investment support is estimated to have increased GDP in the UK in 2015 by 0.1 per cent over and above what it would have been in the absence of the policy, even allowing for the contribution made by the UK to its financing. The evaluation further estimated that GDP will be 0.2 per cent higher in 2023 as a result of the investment concerned.

A UK evaluation for ERDF in England conducted before the end of the 2007–13 period found similar orders of magnitude for job-creation (Regeneris

Table 9.7 Shifts in UK regional eligibility based on 2012–14 GDP per head data.

Region	Eligibility (current)	Eligibility (new)	Change	Population (millions, 2014)
Cumbria	TRANS	MDR	↑	0.50
Cornwall & Isles of Scilly	LDR	TRANS	↑	0.55
Highlands & Islands	TRANS	MDR	↑	0.47
Tees Valley and Durham	TRANS	LDR	↓	1.18
Northumberland, Tyne & Wear	MDR	TRANS	↓	1.43
Derbyshire & Nottinghamshire	MDR	TRANS	↓	2.15
West Midlands	MDR	TRANS	↓	2.81
Essex	MDR	TRANS	↓	1.77
Outer London (East, Northeast)	MDR	TRANS	↓	1.84
Kent	MDR	TRANS	↓	1.78
Dorset & Somerset	MDR	TRANS	↓	1.30
South Western Scotland	MDR	TRANS	↓	2.34

MDR: More-Developed Region; TRANS: Transition Region; LDR: Less-Developed Region.

Source: Bachtler, Mendez & Wishlade (2016).

Table 9.8 Reported values of core indicators of ERDF programmes in the UK, 2007–13 (at end 2014).

Core indicator	Value up to end 2014
Aggregate jobs	152,219
Jobs created	150,339
Number of RTD projects	1,798
Number of enterprise–research institute cooperation projects	7,341
Number of research jobs created	3,877
Number of direct investment aid projects to SMEs	2,344
Number of start-ups supported	52,759
Number of jobs created in SMEs (gross, full time equivalent)	29,124
Kilometres of new roads	13
Kilometres of new TEN-T roads	7
Kilometres of reconstructed roads	11
Kilometres of new railroads	2
Kilometres of TEN-T railroads	2
Kilometres of reconstructed railroads	2
Area rehabilitated (km^2)	1
Number of jobs created in tourism	462

Source: Applica and Ismeri Europa (2016).

2013). Based on programme interim and final evaluations, the analysis concluded that the English ERDF programmes had created around 58,000 gross jobs and safeguarded 59,500 jobs in the period. Project managers expected a further 47,920 jobs to be created by 2013–15 (Tyler 2013). The median ERDF cost per gross job across all programmes was calculated as £23,000 for jobs created and £15,000 for jobs safeguarded – though with wide variation across programmes and projects.

Evaluations of the European Social Fund (ESF) also present a varied picture. Overall, ESF in England is said to have overachieved in terms of the absolute number of results achieved, including 257,000 people gaining basic skills against a target of 201,000; 688,000 participants being in work on exit against a target of 201,000; and 1.1 million being in work six months after exit compared to a target of 238,000 (Kearney & Lloyd 2016). An impact analysis completed in 2011, based on data from the first half of the 2007–13 programme period, suggested that ESF had been successful in contributing towards reducing regional differences in employment rates and skill levels, largely driven by more provision being available in areas with low employment rates, but the impacts on Job Seeker Allowance claimants (the largest claimant group) were small (Ainsworth *et al.* 2011). An evaluation of the net impacts of ESF employment provision on the benefit receipt and employment rate of participants in England found ESF provision to be effective for Incapacity Benefit and Employment Support Allowance participants over the 52 weeks following participation (Ainsworth & Marlow 2011). Positive evaluation findings were also found in Scotland, where a survey of ESF training support for unemployed and economically inactive people was largely an effective route towards employment for participants (Hall Aitken 2012).

Notwithstanding these reported outcomes, meta-reviews of research on the effectiveness of structural funds have not always been conclusive, finding difficulty in identifying the specific contribution of the Funds (Polverari & Bachtler 2014; EPRC 2010). On the one hand, the performance of UK assisted areas over the past two programme periods has been mixed and no significant catching-up can be observed across all regions. Also, additionality is difficult to establish, as structural funds have generally been used in the UK to fund similar forms of intervention to those which are domestically funded, and it is not evident that outcomes and impacts achieved are significantly different than for corresponding activity supported with domestic funding.

On the other hand, research has highlighted several areas where EU structural funds have resulted in economic development activity being expanded, beyond what would have taken place in the absence of EU funding, especially in the Less-Developed Regions (Regeneris 2013; Polverari & Bachtler 2014; Bachtler, Begg, Charles & Polverari 2016; Di Cataldo 2016). The EU programmes have entailed a considerable leverage of other funding sources, especially private funds. They brought a significantly higher level of resources to the UK's Objective 1/Convergence regions and facilitated a more comprehensive effort towards restructuring than is likely to have been made available from any domestic initiative. Thematically, from the mid-1990s, the Funds helped shift the regional development priorities of UK interventions, as well as contributing to the mainstreaming of gender equality, and environmental sustainability, as well as the targeting of community development. The increased focus on financial engineering instruments led to the creation of higher numbers of individual funds (and higher levels of funding) which may be more durable interventions than conventional grant and loan schemes. The Funds also contributed to improved policy-making practices in areas such as strategic planning, partnership-working, monitoring and evaluation.

Overall, however, the challenges that the Funds sought to address in structurally weak regional economies in the UK – low productivity, low entrepreneurship and innovation, high unemployment and worklessness – were so fundamental that EU funding could only be part of the solution. While the Funds had a positive influence, they were often of insufficient magnitude or durability to induce a wider transformation of the regional economy (DCLG

2012; Bachtler *et al.* 2013a; Charles & Michie 2013). However, the reduction or interruption of funding may have major implications for regional economic performance (Di Cataldo 2016; Woolford 2016), which brings us to the question of what UK domestic policies will do to promote regional and local growth following the loss of structural funds.

WHITHER UK REGIONAL POLICY AFTER STRUCTURAL FUNDS?

Regional policy in the UK predates EU structural funds and the UK approach to regional development has continued to evolve independently. It has, though, been influenced in the allocation of resources by the co-funding of EU cohesion policy and in the provision of regional aid by EU Competition Policy control of State aids, as well as other EU regulatory frameworks such as those relating to public procurement and the environment (e.g. the Natura 2000 programme). The challenges for UK policy-makers are whether and how to develop a new approach to spatial imbalances in a new political context and without the guaranteed funding but also obligations of EU cohesion policy.

The post-Brexit political debate has been characterized by discussion of economic and social divisions across age groups, social classes and areas and the appropriate role of government. The UK Prime Minister Theresa May has presented her policy approach as "a country that works for everyone ... built on the values of fairness and opportunity", with specific references to spatial imbalance:

> within our society today, we see division and unfairness all around ... Between the wealth of London and the rest of the country ... [we] need to rebalance the economy across sectors and areas in order to spread wealth and prosperity around the country ... And we will identify the places that have the potential to contribute to economic growth and become the homes to millions of new jobs ... That means inspiring an economic and cultural revival of all of our great regional cities. (May 2016a)

The renamed Department of Business, Energy and Industrial Strategy (DBEIS) and a Cabinet committee for industrial strategy (including the Secretaries of State for 11 departments) are tasked with developing a cross-policy industrial strategy with the stated aim "to put the United Kingdom in a strong position for the future, promoting a diversity of industrial sectors and ensuring the *benefits of growth are shared across cities and regions up and down the country*" (Prime Minister's Office 2016; emphasis added).

146

Of particular note is the (re)emphasis put on "the importance of place" as a principle informing the development of the UK's industrial strategy by the DBEIS Minister, Greg Clark:

> the truth is economic growth does not exist in the abstract. It happens in particular places when a business ... is set up, or takes on more people, or expands its production. And the places in which you do business are a big part of determining how well you can do. And they're very different places ... Yet for too long, government policy has treated every place as if they were identical ... but what is needed in each place is different, and our strategy must reflect that. (Clark 2016)

What this means in practice is still unclear, whether it implies continuity with previous policy statements and commitments, as outlined in the UK "productivity plan" (HM Treasury 2015), or a new direction. Details are being elaborated in a Green Paper on industrial strategy (May 2016b), but, in assessing the regional dimension of the future UK industrial strategy, there are several key issues to consider.

The first concerns the scale of ambition. UK government statements about spatial inequality and the need for rebalancing are not new. The past two decades have seen a succession of White Papers and reviews (see Box 9.1), in each case expressing concern about the overconcentration of economic activity in southeast England, often taking a "year-zero approach" of dismissing the historical policy record as largely ineffective, and asserting that the new policy approach will be radically different. Yet political rhetoric has not been matched by the scale of policy and institutional reform required or the level of resourcing needed. For example, in 2010, the incoming Coalition government's proclaimed need to rebalance the economy was not associated with a greater commitment of resources for regional and local development, which thereafter were on a downward trend.

Over the period from 2010–11 to 2014–15, spending by the UK Government on local growth programmes in England is calculated as £6.2 billion, just over half of the £11.2 billion spent by the regional development agencies over the previous five-year period 2005–06 to 2009–10 (NAO 2013). Lower spending is not confined to England: identifiable spending on enterprise and economic development in Northern Ireland, Scotland and Wales also declined by between 25 and 30 per cent. Future spending commitments will need to take account of whether and how to replace the £10 billion currently allocated to regions through structural funds and crucially whether its regional distribution will follow the EU approach. As Di Cataldo (2016) has

---

Box 9.1 UK Government policy statements on regional policy, 2001–15

Our economy cannot grow as it should while it is so skewed towards London and the south east ... The UK's continued national prosperity depends on cities outside the capital doing better.   HM Treasury (2015)

My proposals are designed to help all regions innovate, grow and increase their absolute wealth. By focusing on raising our performance in every town and city we will return our economy to sustained, long term growth.

Michael Heseltine (2012)

Our economy has become more and more unbalanced, with our fortunes hitched to a few industries in one corner of the country, while we let other sectors like manufacturing slide. Today our economy is heavily reliant on just a few industries and a few regions – particularly London and the South East. This really matters.

David Cameron (2010)

Regional policy is at the heart of our efforts to reach this goal – ensuring that economic prosperity reaches every part of the country and that everyone, no matter where they live, has the chance to make the most of their potential. For too long, too many nations and regions of the United Kingdom have been allowed to fall behind; for too long there have been huge differences in prosperity within regions; and for too long too many people have been left out, their talents wasted.

HM Treasury, Department of Trade and Industry, and
Office of the Deputy Prime Minister (2003)

The new approach will be based on putting greater emphasis on growth within all regions and strengthening the building blocks for economic success by boosting regional capacity for innovation, enterprise and skills development ... Our goal is to increase the rate of growth in all regions by addressing underperformance and building on success.   Department of Trade and Industry (2001)

---

shown in a comparison of funding flows in South Yorkshire and Cornwall, the abrupt downgrading or interruption of funding flows (as occurred in South Yorkshire following the loss of Objective 1 status in 2007) has adverse implications for the promising economic trends in Cornwall, West Wales and other regions benefiting substantially from structural funds.

More fundamentally, as recent analyses of spatial imbalance have noted (Martin *et al.* 2015; McCann 2016), regional inequality cannot be adequately addressed within the existing institutional and policy paradigm – by reconfiguring yet again the mix of business and infrastructure support or the delivery system. Arguably, it requires radical reform and decentralization of the institutional structure comprising the UK's national political economy with respect to governance, finance, taxation and accountability. It is this scale of reform against which the UK's industrial strategy will need to be judged.

A second question is how the rationale and objectives for a place-based industrial strategy are conceptualized. For over 30 years, the primary motivation for UK regional policy has been almost exclusively one of economic efficiency, framed in terms of improving the contribution of regions to national growth and "competitiveness" through investment in support for enterprise, innovation and productivity in regions and cities. The traditional commitments to social justice that underpin EU cohesion policy and many national regional policies in Europe – that individuals have an entitlement to equal living standards and opportunities wherever they live – has been significantly absent. This is reflected in the narrow terms of the regional economic debate in the UK when assessing the scope, justification and effectiveness of the policy or individual measures.

From an international perspective, the UK is something of an outlier (Davies *et al.* 2015). In Germany, the *Grundgesetz* ("basic law") of the Federal Republic mandates the government to pursue a constitutional goal of equivalent living conditions (*gleichwertige Lebensverhältnisse*). This provides the rationale not just for regional economic policy but also fiscal equalization systems to ensure equal access to public services. Regional policy in France is similarly grounded in a constitutional provision requiring government measures "promoting equality between territorial authorities" (MEF 2015). State action under the French policy of *aménagement du territoire* has the objective of increasing regional economic competitiveness but also territorial and social cohesion (*ibid.*). Likewise, the Italian constitution has a commitment to State intervention to promote socio-economic development across the territory to ensure that all citizens, irrespective of where they live, have equal economic and social rights. Thus, regional policy is designed to support both investment and public services, as a means of stimulating more equal economic growth and social opportunities (DSCE 2012; MCT 2014). Regional policies in several other countries – Finland, Norway, Poland, Portugal, Spain, Sweden, Switzerland – have constitutional or policy objectives for balanced development and solidarity that include equal living conditions, access to services, well-being or other aspects of social cohesion. For the UK debate on responses to territorial inequality in the UK, therefore, an important issue is whether social cohesion should similarly be part of the mandate of future regional policy.

149

The third issue for any new approach to regional development in the UK is the spatial institutional framework for addressing inequality and specifically how the lack of coherence in territorial development policy-making can be addressed. Over the past two decades, devolution has transferred powers asymmetrically to Scotland, Northern Ireland and Wales. In England, political and policy-making power remains centralized in London. The deconcentration of policy responsibilities to regional government offices in the 1990s, and subsequently the creation of regional development agencies and (indirectly elected) regional assemblies was reversed over the 2008–12 period with the abolition of all regional governance structures in favour of a "localist" agenda embodied in Local Enterprise Partnerships based on associations of local authorities. England is the only large country in Western Europe that does not have some form of regionalized governance. Across the whole of the UK, local authority powers have also been progressively weakened and subject to more central control over the past four decades.

The UK Government has recently initiated a new phase of devolution in England, notably through the Cities and Local Government Devolution Act 2016 to introduce directly elected mayors to combined local authorities in England and Wales as a basis for devolving housing, transport, planning and policing powers to this new level. Specific initiatives to invest in transport, science and innovation in northern English cities have also been taken under the heading "Northern Powerhouse", and similarly for the Midlands ("Midlands Engine"), and City Deals have been agreed with 28 urban areas across the UK in three waves of support. While welcome as a step towards further devolution and greater focus on structurally weak regions, this English devolution process is still in its early days, will not cover all parts of England, and represents significantly less devolution than to Scotland, Wales and Northern Ireland.

These processes are incentivizing new strategic thinking at urban level in England, but there are important questions about the relationship of the new city regions with the wider regional context, the transparency of resource allocation, the degree of control of city-region administrations over revenue and expenditure, stability across electoral and budgetary cycles, and accountability to local and regional constituencies (Martin *et al.* 2015; O'Brien & Pike 2015). Of particular concern is the position of smaller cities and towns which have long-standing economic development problems dating back (in some cases) to the 1980s which are outside the city regions but are important for particular sub-regional or rural economies. In the absence of a coherent regional framework for planning and implementing economic development, these "economic shadowlands" may be excluded from a city-focused development strategy, lacking the resources to develop their own strategies but also with insufficient political influence and capacity to bid effectively for government funding or make deals.

The mechanisms for coordination and participation are important elements of the emerging structures. One of the underlying principles of cohesion policy is multi-level governance in programming and implementation, requiring (at least in principle) both vertical coordination between different levels of government and horizontal coordination across government departments and with non-government actors. Strategic reference documents at EU and national/sub-national levels provide a framework for the design and delivery of interventions (emulated in some, less prescriptive domestic equivalents at UK and devolved administration levels). The principle of partnership embodied in the EU regulations challenged the centralized, top-down approach to UK regional and industrial development. EU programmes opened the door to local authorities, universities, colleges, environmental organizations, voluntary bodies, employers' groups and trades' unions to be involved in decision-making (at the very least in a consultative capacity) on the design of programmes and delivery of interventions, and (sometimes) selection of projects.

Domestic policy initiatives over the past decade in England have lacked coherence and coordination, as the National Audit Office report on local economic growth in England concluded (NAO 2013). The recent creation of a multi-departmental UK Cabinet committee to govern the approach to industrial strategy may be the start of a more strategic and coordinated approach to territorial development in England, but it begs the question of how other stakeholders will be involved. As O'Brien and Pike (2015: 18) noted with respect to City Deals, they "provide a channel for centre–local communication and relations, potential empowerment of local actors, promotion of local innovation and tailored approaches, and mechanisms for governance reform. However, they note that this approach has also reframed centre–local relations as transactional exchanges" between unequal partners in terms of information, resources and capacity (*ibid.*).

A wider issue is the lack of an institutionalized framework for the UK as a whole. Scotland, Wales and Northern Ireland each have established government structures, but are dealing with difficult strategic questions regarding the relative emphasis given to promoting growth in the key urban centres versus balanced territorial development, as well as the appropriate institutional arrangements for sub-regional involvement in local and regional development. All three parts of the UK share some of the structural problems of northern English regions, and they have significant and (in some cases) widening sub-regional differences in GVA, productivity and employment performance. Structural funds have been an important component in their regional and local development strategies over the long term, and they face important challenges in sustaining positive economic performance in regions such as West Wales or the Highlands & Islands. Further, as illustrated in Table 9.6 above, all three devolved administrations have been active participants in European Territorial Cooperation or other cross-border, inter-regional and transnational networks with EU partners. Although they and other UK authorities could continue to participate in Interreg programmes after Brexit, their involvement would need to be funded wholly from domestic resources, with difficult questions of affordability in continuing engagement as "third-country" partners.

The asymmetric evolution of devolution arrangements has left the UK without well-developed mechanisms for coordinating policy objectives and instruments for territorial imbalance across the constituent parts of the UK or even platforms and networks for sharing information and policy experiences among government authorities beyond structural funds. Again, this contrasts with other European countries which generally have formal or informal coordination and cooperation systems across levels of government both under federal systems (e.g. Austria, Germany, Switzerland) or countries with devolved systems of government (e.g. Italy, Spain).

Lastly, the policy-making process for territorial development needs to be reconsidered. UK policy in this field has often been characterized by the sudden introduction or cessation of regional and local growth policy initiatives for no reason other than changes in political requirements on direction and timing. The consequences are evident in weaknesses in strategy development, objective-setting, implementation planning, performance measurement, evaluation, continuity of funding, transparency and democratic accountability (NAO 2013). EU structural funds have been delivered through multi-annual programmes that provided a stable, predictable investment framework for regional and local organizations that transcended electoral cycles, ministerial changes and short-term domestic budget horizons. Programmes were also obliged to demonstrate a strategic approach to regional challenges, and had to be justified with reference to analysis of territorial strengths and weaknesses. Latterly, for the 2014–20 period, they also had to demonstrate that the preconditions for effective spending were in place (*ex ante* conditionalities), frame objectives with reference to planned outcomes and provide the intervention logic linking the two.

The UK approach also contrasts with the more considered and open policy-making process in the territorial development field of some other European countries. In Germany, regional policy reviews are based on extensive evidence gathering, consultation across government departments and levels of government, and parliamentary hearings before policy changes are introduced. In Norway, policy change is based on a four-year cycle of evaluation, analysis and open consultation leading up to a White Paper. Other countries have similar processes of policy development from which the UK could usefully learn.

CONCLUSIONS

In the wake of the EU referendum vote, the UK Government has the dual problem of managing the UK's exit from the EU – referred to by UK ministers as the "most complex negotiation of all time" – while developing a domestic policy programme capable of responding to profound popular dissatisfaction with economic and social inequality across the UK. The loss of EU structural funds, which have been part of the UK policy landscape for over 40 years, is one consequence of Brexit, and involves important questions as to whether and what kind of domestic regional development approach will take their place at different spatial scales and levels of government.

The disruptive nature of Brexit provides challenges, notably overcoming the loss of EU finance and the desirable parts of its administrative arrangements. This can also be viewed as an opportunity for a substantial transformation of policy and governance that will begin to rebalance the most unequal developed country in Europe. Whether the UK government, in particular (but also the devolved administrations), have the commitment to addressing the fundamental causes of territorial inequality and to implement radical solutions, including the willingness to learn from other models of regional and local development, will be an important determinant of whether the UK really becomes "a country that works for everyone".

ACKNOWLEDGEMENTS

Many thanks to Martin Ferry, Frank Gaskell, Graham Meadows, Rona Michie and Irene McMaster for helpful comments on an earlier version of this paper. Thanks also to DG Regio (Regio-GIS) for Figure 9.2. The usual disclaimer applies.

REFERENCES

ADE 2016. *European Territorial Cooperation: Ex-Post Evaluation of Cohesion Policy Programmes 2007–2013.* WP 11. Report to the European Commission (DG Regio). Brussels: Commission of the European Communities.

Ainsworth, P. & S. Marlow 2011. *Early Impacts of the European Social Fund 2007–13*. London: Department of Work and Pensions.

Ainsworth, P., E. Brooks, E. Cole, S. Marlow & A. Thomas 2011. *European Social Fund Operational Programme 2007–2013: Synthesis of Evidence from the First Half of the Programme*. London: Department of Work and Pensions.

Applica & Ismeri Europa 2016. *WP1: Synthesis Report Ex Post Evaluation of Cohesion Policy Programmes 2007–2013, Focusing on the European Regional Development Fund (ERDF) and the Cohesion Fund (CF)*. Luxembourg: Publications Office of the European Union.

Applica *et al.* 2009. *Ex Post Evaluation of Cohesion Policy Programmes 2000–2006, Co-financed by the European Fund for Regional Development (Objective 1 and 2), Work Package 1: Coordination, Analysis and Synthesis; Task 4: Development and Achievements in Member States; United Kingdom*. Report to the European Commission (DG Regio). Brussels: Commission of the European Communities.

Ashcroft, M. 2016. "How the United Kingdom Voted on Thursday... and Why". 24 November. Retrieved from http://lordashcroftpolls.com/2016/06/how-the-united-kingdom-voted-and-why (accessed 29 December 2016).

Bachtler, J., C. Mendez & F. Wishlade 2013a. *EU Cohesion Policy and European Integration*. Aldershot: Ashgate.

Bachtler J., C. Mendez & F. Wishlade 2013b. *New Budget, New Regulations, New Strategies: The Reform of EU Cohesion Policy*. EoRPA Paper 06/3. Glasgow: European Policies Research Centre, University of Strathclyde.

Bachtler, J., I. Begg, D. Charles & L. Polverari 2016. *EU Cohesion Policy in Practice: What Does It Achieve?* London: Rowman & Littlefield.

Bachtler J., C. Mendez & F. Wishlade 2016. *Evolution or Revolution? Exploring New Ideas for Cohesion Policy 2020+*. EoRPA Paper 16/4. Strathclyde: European Policies Research Centre, University of Strathclyde.

BBC 2016. "EU Referendum: The Result in Maps and Charts". *BBC News* (24 June). Retrieved from www.bbc.co.uk/news/uk-politics-36616028 (accessed 29 December 2016).

Becker, S. O., F. Fetzer & D. Novy 2016. *Who Voted for Brexit? A Comprehensive District-Level Analysis*. CAGE Working Paper 305. Warwick: Centre for Competitive Advantage in the Global Economy, University of Warwick.

Bell, B. & S. Machin 2016. *Brexit and Wage Inequality*. London: Centre for Economic Performance, London School of Economics.

Cameron, D. 2010. "Transforming the British Economy: Coalition Strategy for Economic Growth". Speech delivered 28 May. Retrieved from www.gov.uk/government/speeches/transforming-the-british-economy-coalition-strategy-for-economic-growth (accessed 12 January 2017).

Carozzi, F. 2016. "Brexit and the Location of Migrants". Retrieved from http://spatial-economics.blogspot.co.uk/2016/07/brexit-and-location-of-migrants.html (accessed 29 December 2016).

Charles, D. & R. Michie 2013. *Evaluation of the Main Achievements of Cohesion Policy Programmes and Projects Over the Longer Term in 15 Selected Regions: North East*

England Case Study. Report to the European Commission (DG Regio). Strathclyde: University of Strathclyde.

Clark, G. 2016. "The Importance of Industrial Strategy". Speech by Greg Clark, Secretary of State for Business, Energy and Industrial Strategy, to the Institute of Directors annual conference, 27 September. Retrieved from www.gov.uk/government/speeches/the-importance-of-industrial-strategy (accessed 12 January 2017).

Curtice, J. 2016. "Why did Scotland Vote to Remain? UK in a Changing Europe". Retrieved from http://ukandeu.ac.uk/why-did-scotland-vote-to-remain (accessed 29 December 2016).

Darvas, Z. 2016. "High Inequality and Poverty Helped Trigger the Brexit Protest Vote". Retrieved from http://blogs.lse.ac.uk/brexit/2016/08/31/brexit-should-be-a-wake-up-call-in-the-fight-against-inequality (accessed 29 December 2016).

Darvas, Z. & G. B. Wolff 2016. *An Anatomy of Inclusive Growth in Europe.* Blueprint Series 26. Brussels: Bruegel.

Davies, S. 2016. *Brexit and Regional Disparities in the UK.* EoRPA Policy Briefing. Strathclyde: European Policies Research Centre, University of Strathclyde.

Davies, S., M. Ferry & H. Vironen 2015. *Regional Policy in Europe Targeting Growth and Inequality.* EoRPA Paper 15/1. Strathclyde: European Policies Research Centre, University of Strathclyde.

DCLG 2012. *Government Response to the House of Commons Communities and Local Government Select Committee Second Report of Session 2012–13.* European Regional Development Fund, Department of Communities and Local Government, September, Cm 8389. London: The Stationery Office.

Department of Trade and Industry 2001. *Opportunity for All in a World of Change.* White Paper on Enterprise, Skills and Innovation, Department of Trade and Industry/Department of Education and Employment. London: The Stationery Office.

Di Cataldo, M. 2016. *Gaining and Losing EU Objective 1 Funds: Regional Development in Britain and the Prospect of Brexit.* LSE Europe in Question Discussion Paper Series No.120/2016. London: London School of Economics.

Dorling, D. 2016. "Brexit: The Decision of a Divided Country". *BMJ* **354**: i3697. Retrieved from http://dx.doi.org/10.1136/bmj.i3697 (accessed 29 December 2016).

DSCE 2012. *Rapporto Annuale 2011 DPS sugli interventi nelle aree sottoutilizzate.* Rome: Dipartimento per lo Sviluppo e la Coesione Economica.

EPRC 2010. *Taking Stock of the Effectiveness of Structural Funds Support in the UK.* Final report to Department for Business, Innovation and Skills. Strathclyde: European Policies Research Centre, University of Strathclyde.

European Commission 1987. *European Regional Development Fund: Twelfth Annual Report (1986) from the Commission.* COM (87) 521 final, 1 December. Brussels: Commission of the European Communities.

European Commission 1989. *European Regional Development Fund: Thirteenth Annual Report (1987) from the Commission to the Council, the European Parliament and the Economic and Social Committee.* COM (88) 728 final, 10 January. Brussels: Commission of the European Communities.

European Commission 2011. Europe 2020 targets. Retrieved from http://ec.europa. eu/europe2020/targets/eu-targets/index_en.htm (accessed 29 December 2016).

Eurostat 2016. Eurostat News Release 39/2016, 29 February. Retrieved from http:// bit.ly/1VIJmAi (accessed 29 December 2016).

Goodwin, M. 2016. "Why Britain Backed Brexit: UK in a Changing Europe". Retrieved from http://ukandeu.ac.uk/why-britain-backed-brexit%E2%80%8F (accessed 29 December 2016).

Goodwin, M. & O. Heath 2016. *Brexit Vote Explained: Poverty, Low Skills and Lack of Opportunities.* York: Joseph Rowntree Trust. Retrieved from www.jrf. org.uk/report/brexit-vote-explained-poverty-low-skills-and-lack-opportunities (accessed 29 December 2016).

Hall Aitken 2012. *European Social Fund Participants Survey.* Report to the Scottish Government. Glasgow: Hall Aitken. Retrieved from www.scotland.gov.uk/ Resource/0040/00400347.pdf (accessed 29 December 2016).

Heseltine, M. 2012. *No Stone Unturned in Pursuit of Growth.* London: Department of Business, Innovation and Skills.

HM Government 2012. *United Kingdom National Strategic Report 2012 on the Implementation of the Structural Funds.* London: HM Government.

HM Treasury 2015. *Fixing the Foundations: Creating a More Prosperous Nation.* Cmnd 9098. London: HMSO.

HM Treasury, Department of Trade and Industry & Office of the Deputy Prime Minister 2003. *A Modern Regional Policy for the United Kingdom.* London: HMSO.

Hörnström, L. 2012. *Added Value of Cross-Border and Transnational Cooperation in Nordic Regions.* Nordregio Working Paper 2012:14. Stockholm: Nordic Centre for Spatial Development.

House of Commons 1983. *White Paper: Regional Industrial Development.* Cmnd 9111. London: HMSO.

Kearney, J. & R. Lloyd 2016. *England ESF Programme 2007–2013: Evidence Synthesis.* London: Department of Work and Pensions.

Korski, D. 2016. "Why We Lost the Brexit Vote". *Politico* (20 October). Retrieved from www.politico.eu/article/why-we-lost-the-brexit-vote-former-uk-prime-minister-david-cameron (retrieved 12 January 2017).

McCann, P. 2016. *The UK Regional–National Economic Problem: Geography, Globalisation and Governance.* Abingdon: Routledge.

Martin, R., A. Pike, P. Tyler & B. Gardiner 2015. *Spatially Rebalancing the UK Economy: The Need for a New Policy Model.* Brighton: Regional Studies Association.

May, T. 2016a. "Prime Minister: The Good that Government Can Do". 4 October. Retrieved from http://press.conservatives.com (accessed 29 December 2016).

May, T. 2016b. "CBI Annual Conference 2016: Prime Minister's Speech". 21 November. Retrieved from www.gov.uk/government/speeches/cbi-annual-conference-2016-prime-ministers-speech (accessed 29 December 2016).

Mendez, C., F. Wishlade & J. Bachtler 2013. *A New Dawn for Cohesion Policy? The Emerging Budgetary and Policy Directions for 2014–20*. EoRPA Paper 138/5. Glasgow: European Policies Research Centre, University of Strathclyde.

MCT 2014. *Relazione sull'attività svolta e sulle azioni in corso*. 20 February. Rome: Ministro per la Coesione Territoriale.

MEF 2015. *Projet de loi de finances pour 2016, Annexe: Politique des territoires*. Paris: Ministère de l'économie et des finances.

Mirwaldt, K. & I. McMaster 2008. *Reconsidering Cohesion Policy: The Contested Debate on Territorial Cohesion*. EoRPA Paper 08/5. Strathclyde: European Policies Research Centre, University of Strathclyde.

Mourlon-Druol, E. 2016. "UK Political Elite Used Poverty and Immigration Fears to Secure Leave Vote". Retrieved from http://bruegel.org/2016/06/uk-political-elite-used-poverty-immigration-fears-to-secure-leave-vote (accessed 29 December 2016).

NAO 2013. *Funding and Structures for Local Economic Growth*. London: National Audit Office.

O'Brien, P. & A. Pike 2015. "City Deals, Decentralisation and the Governance of Local Infrastructure Funding and Financing in the UK". *National Institute Economic Review* **233**: 14–26.

Polverari, L. & J. Bachtler 2014. *Balance of Competences Cohesion Review: Literature Review on EU Cohesion Policy*. London: Department for Business, Innovation and Skills.

Prime Minister's Office 2016. "New Cabinet Committee to Tackle Top Government Economic Priority". Press release, 2 August. Retrieved from www.gov.uk/govern ment/news/new-cabinet-committee-to-tackle-top-government-economic-priority (accessed 12 January 2017).

Regeneris 2013. *ERDF Analytical Programme: Workstream 1*. Draft interim report to the Department for Communities and Local Government, February. London: Regeneris Consulting.

Savage, M. & N. Cunningham 2016. "Why Inequality Matters: The Lessons of Brexit". Retrieved from http://items.ssrc.org/why-inequality-matters-the-lessons-of-brexit (accessed 29 December 2016).

SPERI 2016. *UK Regions and European Structural and Investment Funds*. SPERI British Political Economy Brief no. 24. Sheffield: Sheffield Political Economy Research Institute, University of Sheffield.

Tyler, P. 2013. *Expert Evaluation Network Delivering Policy Analysis on the Perform-ance of Cohesion Policy 2007–13, Year 3 – 2013; Task 1: Job Creation as an Indicator of Outcomes in ERDF Programmes, United Kingdom*. Report to the European Commission. Brussels: DG Regio.

Vanhove, N. 1999. *Regional Policy: A European Approach*. Aldershot: Ashgate.

Woolford, J. (2016) "Implications of Brexit for UK ESI Fund Programming and Future Regional Policy". *European Structural and Investment Funds Journal* **4**(3): 144–8.

CHAPTER 10

WHAT DOES BREXIT MEAN FOR THE EUROPEAN UNION?

Tim Oliver

INTRODUCTION

The vote to leave the EU has set in train a series of profound changes to more than just the political economy of the UK: it is an oft-repeated mistake to assume that Brexit is about Britain alone. It is about far more. The vote immediately changed the nature of the EU's relations with the UK, and foreshadows a much deeper change that will shape Britain and Europe once a new relationship – both formal and informal outside the EU – emerges. The vote has also triggered changes within the EU, an often-overlooked aspect of the Brexit debate, which it will be vital to understand. An EU that is different to what we know today, could be the most profound outcome of the Brexit vote. In addition, the vote means a change to the geopolitics of Europe by potentially changing both the UK and the EU and their position within a wider European political network. The vote means one of the core European members of the transatlantic relationship – the UK is its largest and leading European proponent – will no longer be a member of Europe's predominant organization for politics, economics, social and non-traditional security matters.

This raises a series of questions in the USA about the US–UK, US–EU and US–European/NATO relationships. The vote itself, like that of the election of Donald Trump, was viewed as a weathervane of Western political debate, with the outcome seen by some as a sign of a wider and growing rejection of some of the ideas that have defined European politics, transatlantic relations and international relations since 1989: notably a liberal internationalist agenda of sharing sovereignty and viewing globalization and integration as a force for good. Finally, as an unprecedented development for the EU – a *sui generis* organization – the vote raises questions about the nature of European integration and whether the march towards ever-deeper integration has been taken for granted by both policy-makers and academics.

To look at this debate in more detail this chapter examines four topics. They revolve around the 13 Brexit negotiations and debates that are now unfolding in the UK, Europe and elsewhere (Oliver 2016). The negotiations come in three groups: those within the UK, those between the EU and the UK, and those within the remaining EU. Within these exists a fourth set of negotiations that are those between the UK and the remaining EU with the rest of the international community. After some brief discussion of the negotiations unfolding in the UK the chapter focuses largely on developments elsewhere in the EU and around the world. The chapter considers whether Brexit could push the EU towards further integration or disintegration. The chapter ends by asking if Brexit is a crisis for the EU and European integration.

UK BREXIT NEGOTIATIONS

While the focus of this chapter is on what Brexit means for the rest of the EU, we need to briefly recall the negotiations and debates also unfolding within the UK in order to appreciate how the complexity of Brexit could lead to a wider crisis that encompasses the whole of Europe, Britain included. There are five negotiations unfolding within the UK. The first, and most important, is to define the narrative of Brexit (i.e. what the British people voted for and what the UK government's policy on Brexit should reflect). This is not proving easy given the multiple and sometimes conflicting reasons the British people voted for Brexit. Suffice it to say that the debate to define the Brexit narrative has seen the issue of immigration– rightly or wrongly – take pole position. This debate, however, is far from finished and is likely to continue throughout the Brexit negotiations. Second, there will be negotiations and arguments within the main political parties over how to handle Brexit.

Third, the issue of Europe has long divided parties so it should come as no surprise that all the main parties have been trying to come to terms with the outcome with it triggering leadership races in the Conservatives, Labour and UKIP. Given Europe has brought down or haunted several prime ministers and party leaders, we should expect that with Brexit likely to dominate political debate for the next few years it will continue to be an issue that defines and potentially destroys senior political careers. Fourth, negotiations have been unfolding as to who should control and shape the Brexit process in the UK. The decision by the UK's High Court to uphold the right of Parliament to trigger Article 50 was the clearest example so far of the struggle between the government and parliament over who controls the process (FT 2016).

Fifth, the negotiations over who controls Brexit reach beyond Westminster and Whitehall, not least with regard to Scotland, London and Northern

Ireland, all of which voted for Remain. Each will seek to protect their interests in ways that could reshape the UK. Scottish nationalists could use Brexit to push for another Scottish independence referendum. Northern Ireland's peace process has in part been built on the UK and Ireland's shared membership of the EU. London, the political and economic heart of the UK, finds itself a capital city at odds with the country it governs and dominates, a feeling of separation many elsewhere in England have increasingly felt towards it.

Finally, the UK will need to negotiate with its international partners such as the USA, emerging powers and organizations such as NATO and the World Trade Organization (WTO) as it comes to terms with the international and trading implications of leaving the EU. Forging new international relationships will not initially be easy because the focus will be on securing relations with the EU.

EU–UK NEGOTIATIONS

Theresa May's promise that "Brexit means Brexit" sounds, as the *Washington Post*'s Sebastian Mallaby (2016) pointed out, a bit like telling a toddler that "bedtime means bedtime". There will be a bedtime. But as every parent, aunt, uncle, godparent or babysitter experiences at some point, it's never clear when, where and how bedtime will happen. Even the possibility that Brexit might mean "hard Brexit" – bedtime without supper and a story – throws up a host of complex problems. That is in no small part because Brexit does not depend on what Britain wants, it depends on how the rest of the EU reacts and negotiates a Brexit. As such, Brexit is not about Britain but about Europe. It presents a series of complex and until recently largely overlooked or casually dismissed problems for the Union.

The rest of the EU faces four sets of negotiations with the UK over Brexit. The first is that defined by Article 50, which is the exit agreement itself. This will revolve largely around the pensions of existing and former EU officials from the UK, UK contributions to budgets and projects, the status of UK citizens resident elsewhere in the EU and EU citizens resident in the UK, and what to do about MEPs and British staff still serving in EU institutions. While not without difficulty (not least in the remaining costs the UK can expect to pay into and to receive), this will be largely straightforward and plausible within the two-year timeframe set by Article 50. It will be approved by the member states by a qualified majority vote in the European Council after the agreement of the European Parliament has been given.

The real challenge lies in the second negotiation: over the design, scope and approval of a new post-withdrawal UK–EU relationship. This is quite literally a Pandora's box that both sides fear opening. A wide range of new relationships have been proposed and debated, almost exclusively from the UK perspective. What would be a likely offer and best option for the rest of the EU has been largely ignored. This was in part the product of how for a long time the very idea of discussing or analysing an EU member state withdrawing from the Union was a taboo. It conflicted with ideas of the EU as a forward moving, progressive project. Most academic analysis and theoretical models of the EU shared a similar outlook, with little if any contemplation of integration reversing or collapsing. Even when Brexit became a distinct possibility during the referendum campaign, little if any attention was given to contingency planning for a Leave vote. Most debate about new models, for example British membership of the European Economic Area, was conducted within the UK with a view to what was best or worst for the UK. What was best or worst for the EU rarely figured in the analysis. Debate has increased following the vote to leave the EU, but domestic politics such as elections in France and Germany mean debate has remained limited.

A similar lack of analysis had long existed over how the rest of the EU would agree to any new relationship. As any student of the EU's approach to international negotiations knows, it can be a stubborn negotiator because its position often reflects a compromise reached between its 28 members. However, reaching a position in itself is no easy task. While the EU negotiates trade deals on behalf of the whole EU, agreement depends on the member states. As the Transatlantic Trade and Investment Partnership (TTIP) and the Canadian European Trade Agreement (CETA) have shown, securing the agreement of member states is a slow and tortuous process, as each member state has to ratify the deals internally, according to their own domestic legal and political procedures. That the EU – faced with significant political challenges in the Eurozone – has been unwilling to consider a new EU treaty is again a reminder of how unconfident EU decision-makers are that any such treaty would be ratified when it is put before the different member state publics. The rejection of CETA (albeit later overcome) by the parliament of the Belgian region of Wallonia, for example, is a reminder that depending on the type of agreement reached, the Belgian government may have to seek the approval of the country's seven parliaments (Crisp 2016).

Failure to reach any agreement over a new relationship means that at the end of the two years allowed under Article 50, Britain would leave the EU and be left with a relationship with the EU like that of any other WTO member that does not have a trade deal with the EU. WTO membership itself presents some technical challenges to the UK (Mucci, Marks & Oliver 2016). It is also widely considered the least positive relationship for both the UK and the EU.

Furthermore, the lengths of time taken to negotiate agreements such as TTIP (first discussed in the 1990s with formal negotiations ongoing since 2013) or CETA (seven years) serve as a reminder that negotiating and securing agreement over both an exit agreement and a new relationship seems implausible within the two years allowed under Article 50. As several commentators have suggested, to deal with this problem some form of transition relationship may be required, for example membership of the European Economic Area (Chalmers & Menon 2016). What that transition period may look like, how long it would last, and how it would be agreed (both in the EU and UK) remains open to speculation.

The EU has so far met Brexit with a resolve to remain united. The 27 member states and the EU institutions have refused to negotiate Brexit in advance of Article 50 being triggered by the British government. In part that reflects an awareness that once the two-year clock set down in Article 50 is started then the rest of the EU has leverage over a UK desperate to secure some kind of deal. An extension can be agreed, but as set out in Article 50 this would require the unanimous consent of the UK and the rest of the EU. The EU's refusal to negotiate also reflects, however, an awareness that the UK will attempt 27 different negotiations. While we should not overplay Britain's ability to divide and rule in its attempts to secure a deal, the EU knows from negotiating with other countries such as Russia, the USA or Turkey that internal divisions can leave it weak and divided. In the UK it faces its most formidable external partner: a country with over forty years of experience at working the corridors of Brussels and which will become the EU's largest trading partner, to say nothing of the security and political relations that will exist in some way. It is worth remembering that the UK's economic place in the EU is substantial and while this does not mean the EU needs the UK more than Britain needs the EU, as some British Eurosceptics often argue, it does mean the rest of the EU faces a cost from Brexit. Britain constitutes 17.6 per cent – or around one sixth – of the EU's economic area (Irwin 2015), with 12.8 per cent of its population (Eurostat 2016). British exports were 19.4 per cent of the EU's total exports in 2012 (excluding intra-EU trade) (Open Europe 2012). Within the EU Britain runs a large trade deficit with the rest in goods and services, around £28 billion a year in 2011 and as high as £61.6 billion in 2014 (Hansard 2012; ONS 2015). While for the time-being the UK lacks even the full complement of diplomats and negotiators to handle Brexit and associated trade deals, its place as the EU's biggest trading partner does give it some leverage, not least with those countries that do face an economic cost from UK–EU relations reverting to a WTO relationship.

Brexit will therefore be a test of the EU's ability to negotiate within itself a complex deal that not only threatens to divide it in terms of competing national interests, but which challenges some of the founding ideas of the EU (Brexit being a challenge to the idea of "ever closer union"), faces significant institutional constraints, and where any one of 27 domestic political games could wreak havoc on the negotiations (Oliver 2015). Managing this will be no easy undertaking for those tasked with leading the EU side of the negotiations. Each of the various EU institutions have appointed Brexit teams led by high profile individuals. The European Commission's team is led by Michel Barnier, a former French minister. It is unclear how his team will relate to that of the European Council, but it is likely they will undertake most of the detailed background work. Key decisions will surround the European Council, representing the member states. Didier Seeuws, an experienced Belgian diplomat, will lead a task force for the Council, coordinating with UK negotiators over the most sensitive parts of the Brexit negotiations. Informally the Council's position – and therefore the dominant partner on the EU side of negotiations – will be shaped by certain member states more than others, especially the larger states of Germany and France. Significant efforts will also made by others who could be most affected such as Ireland, the Netherlands, Poland and Scandinavian states. Britain will find itself negotiating with these multiple actors individually at the same time as they caucus to try and reach agreement over an EU position. Into this we also need to factor in the European Parliament, which will be required to approve any exit deal. Its appointment of Guy Verhofstadt, a former Belgian prime minister who is deeply committed to further integration, was a clear signal it considers issues of European unity to be the foremost concern. Given the long history in British politics of politicians and media dismissing and ridiculing the European Parliament, it is easy to foresee a situation in which its powerful place in the EU is once again overlooked and snubbed.

BREXIT, DIPLOMACY, SECURITY AND DEFENCE

In the first few months after the Brexit vote, attention among some policy-makers and think-tank researchers in the rest of the EU turned to how other large countries manage relations with a smaller but not insignificant neighbouring partner. Two obvious examples are the US–UK and US–Canadian relationships. Indeed, the idea that Britain might become the EU's Canada, or the lesser half of a second "special relationship", has been joked about in Brussels. Such jokes overlook the fragility of the EU compared to the USA. They do, however, show that beyond talk of transition agreements or EU–UK trade deals, some form of close political bond and network will need to be forged or singled out from existing relations. At heart this will be about what the UK and EU can fall back on as a solid bond that unites the two and weathers any Brexit storm. In looking to the US–UK and US–Canadian relationships, European policy-makers and researchers will have noted the central role of security and defence cooperation in any international coalition. The US–UK "special relationship" is at heart special because of almost inseparable relations in three areas: nuclear weapons, intelligence sharing and special forces. That is the core of the relationship that continues irrespective of – and is often protected from – political disagreements over economics or other matters.

Whether the UK and EU can find a way forward in security and defence cooperation depends on the five ways in which Brexit could shape the UK's defence and security arrangements: it could alter the composition of the UK and the placement of its defence capabilities (secession of Scotland, home to Trident, could bring to an end Britain's nuclear deterrent, and naval facilities in Gibraltar could be lost given the future of the territory has been thrown into doubt by it voting remain due to its overwhelming links to Spain); a smaller economy would inevitably reduce the amount spent on defence in real terms; diplomatic and defence relationships between the UK and the rest of the world will need to be reworked, as extrication from the EU will require more staff, resources and expertise than has recently been delegated to the EU; and without the UK, the EU may develop its own independent defence capabilities.

Since its founding the importance of NATO has been central to UK defence policy. Britain's commitment to NATO has not been questioned by the vote to leave the EU, although there have been some rumours that Ministers have considered using Britain's commitment to NATO as leverage in Brexit negotiations (Grant 2016). Instead Britain might place increasing emphasis on NATO as the forum through which it engages in pan-European security and political matters. This could clash with the EU's own efforts at giving the Union a defence and security capability. While such efforts may be over-hyped, and perhaps an ill-thought through reaction to Brexit, they demonstrate that the EU is the predominant economic and political actor in Europe. Britain will struggle to avoid this and like the USA need to ensure relations with Europe are not narrowly pursued through a NATO framework alone. In the short-term Britain's existing bilateral defence relations with France, Denmark, the Netherlands and Norway will remain unaffected. But this depends on what becomes of the EU. Should it find unity and develop into a significant power in defence and security then the UK could find it faces the one thing British governments have long sought to avoid: a single power dominating the European continent (Blagden 2016). Granted, given the EU's current state of affairs and the state of European defence expenditure such a development seems a distant possibility. The UK is one of only four European states to meet the NATO defence spending guidelines of 2 per cent of GDP, the others being Estonia, Greece and Poland. Overall NATO defence spending averages only 1.18 per cent of GDP per member (NATO 2016). This has led to criticisms that the 2 per cent guideline is failing and that it overlooks other contributions. That even the UK has been accused of some creative accounting to reach the 2 per cent serves as a reminder of the difficulties Europe faces in increasing defence spending. Despite this, minus the UK the EU would lose one of its two serious military powers, the other being France. Should European states ever get their act together on defence in a way that leads to a more coherent EU defence capability then the EU would become a benign dominant power compared to those the UK has faced– and feared – in the past. Despite this, such a development would confront the UK with a radically different Europe and transatlantic relationship than that which it has been accustomed to.

IMPLICATIONS FOR THE EUROPEAN UNION

The idea of the EU becoming a United States of Europe – and therefore the defining power of Europe – can seem absurd when we consider how Brexit is one of several significant challenges facing it. As Rem Korteweg (2015) argued, the EU can appear to be surrounded by the four horsemen of the apocalypse: war haunts Ukraine and Eastern Europe; Death harvests refugees and migrants in the Mediterranean; Famine brings hardship to Greece and other struggling Eurozone economies; while Pestilence in the form of Euroscepticism spreads around Europe, claiming its first victim in the form of Britain. Viewing the EU in such a state of crisis can appear extreme, but it does convey how Brexit cannot be seen alone but as part of a wider series of challenges facing the EU.

The loss of the UK will lead to a changed balance of power within the EU, which will be at the forefront of decision-makers' minds as they negotiate Brexit. Inevitably, countries – and especially certain governments – that have aligned with Britain on matters of policy, economics or ideology may contemplate a new relationship with Britain that affords the UK more influence over internal EU politics than those more distant would prefer to grant it. There is a possible shift away from Western Europe towards a Union that is more concerned with the outlook of countries in Eastern Europe. The withdrawal of a country which has pursued deregulation and liberal economics may be used as an opportunity by governments and other actors to push the EU more towards a protectionist set of economic policies. The power of the EU's institutions will also come into play. As noted earlier, the European Parliament and Commission have each taken a proactive approach to Brexit negotiations in no small part to assert themselves within the political tug of war that has long existed in Brussels between the EU institutions and the member states. As the supranational institutions of the EU, they fear the Council and member states – and especially the larger ones – will agree a deal among themselves and with Britain that they then expect the institutions to accept. This would be a development the Parliament would strongly resist, signalling as it would the assertion of the Council as the EU's preeminent decision-making body. As always in EU politics, the place of Germany, and the effects of Brexit on the Franco–German axis, will be the focus of much discussion. Focus will fall on whether Brexit has made the EU more German or weakened Germany's position thanks to losing an ally with whom it has sometimes aligned itself.

Britain's reputation for being an awkward partner in the EU might lead to a conclusion that its departure will make reform of the Union easier. The past few years have seen growing demands for change to the EU, possibly through treaty change. David Cameron had hoped his plans for a renegotiation of the UK's place in the EU would align with a wider effort to change the Union. However, such hopes should be set against Britain's declining influence within the EU over the past few years. Events such as Cameron's veto of a proposed new treaty in 2011 might point to a future where such an obstacle will be absent allowing the EU to move forward, but in 2011 the rest of the EU quickly found a way around the UK by agreeing an intergovernmental treaty among themselves. This is not to argue that Britain has not been a leading player in the EU (Daddow & Oliver 2016). The Janus-faced attitude of successive governments – a private constructive attitude in Brussels but poisonous, Eurosceptic debate in Britain – has often bewildered European commentators. The past few years have, however, seen Britain play a declining and peripheral role. This in part reflects how because of crises and the growing centrality of Germany, the Eurozone has become the heart of the Union, excluding the UK thanks to its non-membership. It also reflects growing levels of Euroscepticism in Britain that, in one of the clearest examples, pushed the Conservative Party and David Cameron to disconnect from Europe's mainstream and governing centre-right Christian Democrat parties. Britain's ability to influence and obstruct the EU has therefore diminished. While the unwanted task of Brexit poses significant challenges, and British ministers have hinted at using the threat of disrupting EU decision-making as a way of leveraging a better Brexit deal, there will come a time when the rest of the EU can no longer blame the UK for directly disrupting or blocking integration and EU business.

This is not to say, however, that Britain will not attempt to disrupt or shape EU decision-making from the outside. As noted above, upon leaving the EU Britain will move from being a decision-maker to decision-shaper, and potentially one of the most influential should the British business community and civil society continue to lobby heavily in Brussels. This will in part reflect Britain's continued close economic relationship with the rest of the EU. It will also reflect that Britain will remain one of the largest states in Europe. Even if the UK were to break-up, England's current population of 55 million is expected to continue growing with Britain on course to overtake Germany's declining population before the middle of the century (Eurostat 2011). Population alone, of course, is no guarantee of power and influence and Brexit may undermine such projections for the UK. That said, Britain's move to the outside of the EU could reinforce the emergence of a Europe that is being torn in different directions, what has been termed a "multipolar Europe" with Turkey and Russia as the other two European poles (Krastev & Leonard et al. 2010). Brexit adds – or perhaps makes clearer – another pole, this time in Western Europe. Unless the EU develops in ways that strengthen its unity these three poles could pull it in different directions, for example Russia pressuring Eastern Europe and Germany and Britain pulling in the West, to say nothing of the tensions China or the USA could exert.

Finally, Brexit has raised questions about whether the EU will disintegrate. The term "dis-integration" is slightly misleading given it is unclear what the Union would become. Even if the EU were to be replaced with a Europe of nation-states that lack a predominant overarching supranational organization and institutions, there would continue to be organizations such as NATO, the Council of Europe, the Organization for Security and Co-operation in Europe and a multitude of other regional and multilateral organizations that connect Europe's states (or groups of them) together. Disintegration could therefore turn out to lead to a reduced or reordered EU, perhaps focused on a few core countries in a rump Eurozone surrounding Germany. How European disintegration would unfold and what might trigger it has rarely been the subject of much analysis, a reflection in part of a view of European integration as a forward moving, liberal internationalist project (see Vollaard 2014; Webber 2014).

For Webber, one of the most important aspects of any disintegration would be the response of the EU's predominant power and (reluctant) leader: Germany. Managing Germany's place in Europe has been a central part of European integration (and NATO) since it began. German reunification in 1990 was a key driver behind the creation of the Euro, with Germany sacrificing the Deutschmark as a way to bind the reunified Germany into Europe as a "European Germany" so as to assuage fears (including in Britain) of a "German Europe". Since then Germany's place as the heart of the EU – physically, politically, economically, ideologically and as its paymaster – has grown. This has created expectations of leadership that have not been easy for a German people or political elite that also fear the creation of a "German Europe". Brexit has increased the calls for German leadership by adding to the pressures facing the EU that require Berlin to take action to resolve. The departure of a large member state like Britain also enhances Germany's centrality in the remaining EU. Germany's central place in the EU therefore makes it central to any ideas of European disintegration. The EU has never, as Webber argues, faced a "crisis made in Germany". Webber is unclear as to what such a crisis might entail, but it is likely to be one where the German government and people lose faith in the current EU project as a result of a widespread breakdown in EU solidarity and the increasing costs Germany is asked to carry in order to maintain the EU's unity and existing setup. Brexit alone is unlikely to trigger this, but if problems in the Brexit negotiations aligned with another crisis in the Eurozone or Schengen then the approach the EU has so far taken of muddling through each separate crisis could prove unsustainable (Wright 2013).

BREXIT: A EUROPEAN CRISIS?

The multiple players and playing fields of Brexit and the numerous ways in which Brexit could be enabled or constrained has led some to conclude that Brexit won't happen or that it constitutes such a crisis for the UK, the EU or both that it would be dangerous for either side to push forward with it. It is possible to imagine a "harsh Brexit" which sees a breakdown in trust between the various actors leading to a deterioration in relations between some or all involved, ending in significant damage (potentially a break-up) of the UK, the EU or both (Morillas 2016). That said, even a harsh Brexit could amount to a crisis that forces all involved to realize what they have to lose. The outcome could be what can be termed a "harsh-positive" Brexit in which instead of muddling through Brexit – coping with it rather than solving the problems it presents – the EU and UK are confronted with such a crisis that they are forced to find a viable way forward.

Is Brexit therefore a crisis for the UK and/or the EU? Politics is the daily management of crises, and in some ways Brexit takes the long running problems of UK–EU relations to a new level. In doing so Brexit can be said to meet the definition of a crisis as something that is dramatic, vivid, emotionally charged and carrying significant consequences. Crises are moments or periods of truth which test leaders and the robustness of political institutions, and in which frailties are revealed, in no small part because the limited time available limits the opportunities for adaptation (Rosenthal, Boin & Comfort 2001). Crises capture the attention of leaders, commentators and analysts, and so risk neglecting other big but less exciting problems.

Brexit is testing the robustness of both the EU and the UK as political unions, and threatens some of the goals either side have set whether it be "ever closer union" or the idea of Britain as a great power. The time available is limited by the domestic, political, legal and economic demands both sides face, not least for the UK. Extending the time available could lessen any sense of crisis, albeit at the risk of triggering a backlash from those – in both the UK and the rest of the EU – who would like to see the process happen quicker whatever the cost. All sides are in the early stages of feeling their way forward with an unprecedented problem. The potential for unexpected surprises remains high; not least that one actor somewhere along the way in one of the above negotiations – for example, a vote in a parliament or a legal challenge – could disrupt the entire process.

Any sense of crisis might appear more applicable to the UK than to the EU. However, this would be to overlook the part Brexit plays in a potentially transformative period in the EU's development, potentially a period that sees its unravelling or reconfiguration. In writing about the future of the EU in overcoming the Eurozone crisis, Thomas Wright (2013) of Brookings wrote of three paths forward for the EU: integration, muddling through, or disintegration. Given the Eurozone crisis is an on-going problem for the EU, one it has so far muddled through rather than solved, it seems probable that it will face Brexit in much the same way unless a major crisis arises. Here it is worth recalling that the EU has tended to integrate when faced with a major crisis, with even the muddling through response to the Eurozone crisis bringing with it a degree of further integration. Instead of muddling through, Brexit may – as one of a series of problems it faces – push the EU towards a defining moment or event that necessitates a large step forward in integration. With populism on the rise across Europe, however, that moment may not necessarily lead to further integration but instead to decline and disintegration of the EU as we have known it.

REFERENCES

Blagden, D. 2016. "The Fate of Britain: Offshore Balancing and the Brexit". 28 April. Retrieved from http://warontherocks.com/2016/04/the-fate-of-britain-offshore-balancing-and-the-brexit (accessed 30 December 2016).

Chalmers, D. & A. Menon 2016. *Getting Out Quick and Playing the Long Game*. Briefing 07/2016. London: Open Europe. Retrieved from http://openeurope.org.

uk/intelligence/britain-and-the-eu/3-step-brexit-solution (accessed 30 December 2016).

Crisp, J. 2016. "Brexit: Canada's Trade Model is Not a Golden Ticket to the Single Market". *New Statesman,* 14 October. Retrieved from www.newstatesman.com/ politics/brexit/2016/10/brexit-canadas-trade-model-not-golden-ticket-single-market (accessed 30 December 2016).

Daddow, O. & T. Oliver 2016. "A Not So Awkward Partner: The UK Has Been a Champion of Many Causes in the EU". 15 April. Retrieved from http://blogs.lse. ac.uk/brexitvote/2016/04/15/a-not-so-awkward-partner-the-uk-has-been-a-champion-of-many-causes-in-the-eu (accessed 30 December 2016).

Eurostat 2011. "Population Projections 2010–2060". 8 June. Retrieved from http:// europa.eu/rapid/press-release_STAT-11-80_en.htm (accessed 12 January 2017).

Eurostat 2016. "Population Change: Demographic Balance and Crude Rates at National Level". July. Retrieved from http://appsso.eurostat.ec.europa.eu/nui/ show.do?dataset=demo_gind&lang=en (accessed 12 January 2017).

FT 2016. "Article 50 High Court Ruling: Extracts". *Financial Times* (3 November). Retrieved from www.ft.com/content/d8d3a14a-a1bf-11e6-aa83-bcb58d1d2193 (accessed 30 December 2016).

Grant, C. 2016. "Theresa May and Her Six-Pack of Difficult Deals". 28 July. Retrieved from www.cer.org.uk/insights/theresa-may-and-her-six-pack-difficult-deals (accessed 30 December 2016).

Hansard 2012. "Answer from Baroness Warsi". 14 November, c1507. Retrieved from www.theyworkforyou.com/lords/?id=2012-11-14a.1507.0 (accessed 30 December 2016).

Irwin, G. 2015. *Brexit: The Impact on the UK and the EU.* London: Global Counsel. Retrieved from www.global-counsel.co.uk/system/files/publications/Global_ Counsel_Impact_of_Brexit_June_2015.pdf (accessed 30 December 2016).

Korteweg, R. 2015. *The Four Horsemen Circling the European Council Summit.* 24 June. London: Centre for European Reform.

Krastev, I. & M. Leonard with D. Bechev, J. Kobzova & A. Wilson 2010. *The Spectre of a Multipolar Europe.* London: European Council on Foreign Relations.

Mallaby, S. 2016. "Britain's Post-Brexit Warning for Americans Seduced by Trump". *Washington Post* (1 September). Retrieved from www.washingtonpost.com/ opinions/global-opinions/britains-post-brexit-warning-for-americans-seduced-by-trump/2016/09/01/829f7770-704d-11e6-9705-23e51a2f424d_story.html (accessed 30 December 2016).

Morillas, P. 2016. *The Brexit Scenarios: Towards a new UK–EU Relationship.* June. Barcelona: CIDOB. Retrieved from www.cidob.org/en/publications/publication_ series/documents_cidob_new_era/the_brexit_scenarios_towards_a_new_uk_ eu_relationship (accessed 30 December 2016).

Mucci, A., S. Marks & C. Oliver 2016. "Forget Brussels, Brexit's Toughest Battleground is the WTO". 8 October. Retrieved from www.politico.eu/article/forget-brussels-brexits-toughest-battleground-is-the-wto-uk-theresa-may (accessed 30 December 2016).

NATO 2016. "Defence Expenditure of NATO Countries (2008–2015)". Press release, 28 January. Retrieved from www.nato.int/nato_static_fl2014/assets/pdf/pdf_2016_01/20160129_160128-pr-2016-11-eng.pdf (accessed 30 December 2016).

Oliver, T. 2015. "How the EU Responds to a British Withdrawal Will be Determined by Five Key Factors". 3 December. Retrieved from http://blogs.lse.ac.uk/brexitvote/2015/12/03/europes-potential-responses-to-a-british-withdrawal-from-the-union-will-be-determined-by-ideas-interests-institutions-the-international-and-individuals (accessed 30 December 2016).

Oliver, T. 2016. "Brexit is About Britain, Not Europe". 13 October. Retrieved from http://ukandeu.ac.uk/brexit-is-about-europe-not-britain/

ONS 2015. "How Important is the European Union to UK Trade and Investment?". 26 June. Retrieved from http://webarchive.nationalarchives.gov.uk/20160105160709/www.ons.gov.uk/ons/rel/international-transactions/outward-foreign-affiliates-statistics/how-important-is-the-european-union-to-uk-trade-and-investment-/sty-eu.html (accessed 30 December 2016).

Open Europe 2012. *Right Speech, Right time?* London: Open Europe.

Rosenthal, U., R. A. Boin & L. K. Comfort 2001. *Managing Crises: Threats, Dilemmas, Opportunities*. Springfield, IL: Charles C. Thomas.

Vollaard, H. 2014. "Explaining European Disintegration". *Journal of Common Market Studies* **52**(5): 1142–59.

Webber, D. 2014. "How Likely is it That the European Union Will Disintegrate? A Critical Analysis of Competing Theoretical Perspectives". *European Journal of International Relations* **20**(2): 341–65.

Wright, T. 2013. "Europe's Lost Decade". *Survival* **55**(6): 7–28.

INDEX

Note: italic page numbers indicate figures and tables; numbers in brackets preceded by *n* are footnote numbers.